TODAY

BREE GROFF

WAS FUN

A BOOK ABOUT WORK (SERIOUSLY)

PAGE
TWO

Quotations from Milton Glaser recounted in his conversations with
Sue Walsh are included with the permission of the Glaser family and estate.

Some names and identifying details have been changed
to protect the privacy of individuals.

The views in this book are those of the author alone and
do not necessarily represent the views of SYPartners
or any other organization with which the author is affiliated.

Cataloguing in publication information is
available from Library and Archives Canada.
ISBN 978-1-77458-559-7 (paperback)
ISBN 978-1-77458-566-5 (ebook)

Page Two
pagetwo.com

Page Two™ is a trademark owned by Page Two Strategies Inc.,
and is used under license by authorized licensees.

Cover design by Rodrigo Corral
Interior design by Peter Cocking
Printed and bound in Canada by Friesens
Distributed in Canada by Raincoast Books
Distributed in the US and internationally by Macmillan

25 26 27 28 29   5 4 3 2 1

breegroff.com

for

Brad, my favorite coworker

Arden, my favorite deliverable

my mom and dad, the best bosses I ever had

thank you for all the fun days

CONTENTS

INTRODUCTION

Hi there, my name is Bree.

And I know for a fact that work can be fun.

My mom was a kindergarten teacher who spent decades teaching in room 109 at Hamilton Elementary School in Chicago. Starting when I was seven years old, whenever I had a day off school that she didn't, I would head into work with her as her assistant teacher. It was my first "job." Sure, the work was unpaid and acquired through nepotism and not really a job at all, but it was glorious! I thought up fun ways to teach handwriting. I was sent on important errands around the school. The kids all wanted to hang around me. I felt creative and useful and loved.

My mom had her ups and downs at work like any of us, but what I remember most is her coming home and saying, "I have the best days." I can still hear her voice now as I type this.

My dad was the principal at Portage Park Elementary School. What I remember most about visiting his school was how much he laughed with his colleagues. They looked like friends. I remember the fishing trips he would go on with the building engineer. Even after he retired, he and other school retirees would meet for monthly lunches simply because they enjoyed each other.

In other words, I grew up seeing that work was a place to have fun!

Well IMAGINE MY SURPRISE years later when I learned about 50-page slide decks with 10-point font, a standard two weeks of vacation, and not having time to pee between meetings.

What the hell is this?!

So much about the working world seemed patently ridiculous, if not outright dangerous. It's not normal to not eat all day because you're running from one thing to the next. It's not normal to be up in the middle of the night worrying about an upcoming meeting. It's not normal to devote the best parts of yourself to a job and then wonder if anything you did at work made an impact. It's not normal to look at email before you look at the partner lying next to you in bed every morning. It's not normal to forgo exercising and doctor's appointments because they're just too hard to fit in. It's not normal to see kids and partners as distractions from work ("Sorry honey, I'm in the middle of this thing."). It's not normal to choose being high performing over happy. And it's definitely not normal to wish away the workweek ("Just gotta get to Friday!") when what we are really doing is wishing away five-sevenths of our lives.

Except that all of those things are perceived as being *entirely normal.*

I have lived this existence! Perhaps you have lived it, or are living it, too.

I'm not here to swing the pendulum from workaholism to "down with work." Nor am I here to help leaders figure out how to get more work from their employees through the guise of engagement. I'm here to settle the pendulum in the center. Work should be a source of joy because it's fundamentally good, *and* it should be only one of many joys in our lives.

The prevailing opinion about work is that it's, well, *work.* Behind every comment about being exhausted by Friday is a belief that work is extractive; that we empty ourselves for our employers in exchange for money; that we grin and bear the exhaustion so we can refill ourselves on our own time.

Most people faced with a terminal illness would eagerly trade all their dollars if it meant more time with their friends and family. And yet, in health, we so often trade our time with friends and family for money—and as we do, we wish away our days.

Indeed, we work for money. Everyone needs a living wage, and making that a reality is a book for a socioeconomic expert to write. What I've become fascinated by is why those who earn enough for the necessities of life are *still* unhappy in their work, their life, or both.

It's not any one person that's stuck in this trap. It's a system, a culture, a lexicon, a shared belief that "work sucks" and we spend our time the way we're told. In childhood, school bells drive our days, and when we grow up, our calendars become our overlords. We start to use words like "time off" and "break" as if work is our default mode and any time not working is time "away." We ask each other if we feel refreshed after coming back from a "well-deserved" vacation as if the vacation existed only in relation to work: a reward for a job well done, or a means of refueling to do more work upon our return.

What a terrible way to think about our lives *and* our work!

I don't want it to be that way, and I dare say, you don't want it that way either. Perhaps surprisingly, companies shouldn't either, and they're catching on. The number of consulting engagements about culture, employee experience, and the future of work has skyrocketed. While the war for talent may ebb and flow with the unemployment rate, the battle for top talent is always hot. The irony is that if individuals are given the opportunity to work and live intentionally, organizations might realize they had top talent all along—that their people were just tired and a little resentful before.

I see a better way. It looks something like this:

In early March of 2020, my team and I were preparing for a big in-person client session. The client asked if we could do it virtually, which seemed terribly conservative given this virus was going to come and go by April. But we obliged and diligently dug in over the next week, converting our big 3D plans into pixels. Two of our team members got so good at the fancy functionality of our virtual tools that we appointed Chad "Zoom Dood," and Josh became "Slido Guy."

That week as we worked we talked about our designer Sasha's time in culinary school and Chad's daughter and Matt K.'s dog. Our program manager, Carrie, who later went on to become a social worker, used her talents to keep us cool amidst chaos. As the days went on, the number of people in the office fell, which meant the number of days I wore stretchy pants rose. On the day of the session, I wore a cashmere sweater and full-on pajama pants, because why the hell not. And after, we went to a probably ill-advised lunch, but as Matt B. and I agreed recently, that was the best meal we've had at work. All joy.

That week I wasn't stressed because I knew that we had it. I looked forward to going home at night to see Brad and Arden, and then I looked forward to going to work again the next day to see the team. I laughed a lot. And at the end of each day, do you know what I said to myself?

Today was fun!

And the work was a grand success too. Over the years our main client, Caroline, became a great friend. We've met each other's families and gone to the beach together, and she's been amazingly supportive of me both professionally and personally.

 This was us:

I loved this team, but since I've been a part of so many more like this one, I know it's not a happy accident. We can design our teams and our work for great days. I've tried over the years to capture how exactly I know how to do this, but one day I made myself sit my butt down and start writing. The results of that were my seven rules for better days that are the framework for this book, and which I'll talk more about in the wayfinding section that follows.

So now you know about my work philosophy, my parents, and my affinity for spandex, but perhaps I should throw a few credentials around, too.

Since I didn't formally introduce myself before, I'm Bree Andrea (née Berman) Groff.

I have focused my career on organizational transformation, employee experience, and the future of work, partnering with leaders at Pfizer, Microsoft, Calvin Klein, Atlassian, Hilton, and Alphabet, among many others. I love sharing my learnings on a stage and have delivered dozens of keynotes around the globe on change and the human experience of work.

I am a senior advisor to the transformation consultancy SYPartners, which for the past 30+ years has been working to create organizations and a world of work that are driven by humanity as much as performance. Previously, I was the CEO of NOBL Collective, a global organizational design and change consultancy pioneering new ways of working.

I have founded and led an innovation department, advised leaders as a service designer, and researched body language while working in the R&D department of a dating app company. In a previous career, I taught middle and high school math and physics, and before that, I was an undoubtedly unsuccessful LA actor. I hold a BA from the University of Pennsylvania and an MS in organizational learning and change from Northwestern University.

But that's just work—and it's not everything. I have a super handsome and brilliant husband named Brad and a talented and hilarious daughter named Arden (10 years old when this book launches). I'm lucky to see my dad almost every day since my beautiful mom passed away. When I'm stressed, my motto is "most things, most days," and sometimes that means ending my day in bed eating takeout queso and watching reality TV. But most days, I'm healthy. Most days I'm happy. Most days I have a really, really good time at work.

All of these different experiences mean I see work through a multifaceted lens. I've had the privilege of partnering with many different CEOs and CHROs and interviewing a vast array of their people, which allows me to peek into their cultures and develop broad pattern recognition. I learn from the teams I lead, as well as other colleagues who come to me to discuss both the joys of work and the effects of overwork. I've supported many leaders with big mandates and was once a CEO myself.

I know the pressure a business and its leaders face to make money—not for reasons of greed, but simply to keep the business healthy. I hear both "kids these days" and "stick it to the man" arguments among many "I'm just trying to do my best" sentiments.

These experiences have given me a rich perspective on what work is, who it's for, and what it looks like at its best. Though many of the learnings in this book come from these professional experiences, what has meant the most—and where I have learned the most—is my own grappling with how I want to spend my days.

In January 2022, I learned that my mother had terminal cancer. As an only child, I took immediate leave from work and devoted myself to her care, as well as that of my dad, who already had Alzheimer's. Sometimes it takes sitting in the waiting room at a cancer center with beautiful humans yearning for more days to see the absurdity of wishing them away.

That's why I'm writing this book, in the hopes that it helps you love your days.

Even Monday to Friday.

Wayfinding

I'll note upfront that this isn't your average business book. The vast majority of business books are designed to *tell*, not show—properly outlining their arguments with the occasional research and anecdotes. But we are more than reasoning machines! I could not bring myself to drone on about humanity and fun without also showing up in all my humanity and inviting some fun.

Together we'll go on a journey in two parts, across seven rules for having more good days.

PART ONE: WORK SHOULD BE A SOURCE OF JOY...

PART TWO: ...ONE OF MANY IN OUR LIVES

You'll note that nested within each chapter are two sections: the first makes the case for the chapter's key idea, and the second offers more practical mindsets, exercises, and tools.

Finally, in addition to sharing some good old-fashioned research and client examples, I'll invite you to play music, try to make you laugh, give you a token to carry around, and offer a puzzle to solve. There will be exercises for leaders endeavoring to make work better, along with practices for individuals. I'll show up as myself, not some professional behind a curtain. There will be poetry. Memes. Field trip invitations. All diverse, yet cohesive.

Let's begin!

PART ONE

WORK SHOULD BE A SOURCE OF JOY...

1

MOST WORK, MOST DAYS, SHOULD BE FUN

I've got the "Sunday Scaries."

Ugh, Mondays are the worst.

Is it only Wednesday?

TGIF!

It's a refrain so common we don't bother to question it. Kids don't make it to second grade without picking up the tune. But why should it be that way? Why should we wish away our lives until we retire?

We don't need to continue working as we have been. We don't need to spend Saturdays recovering from work and Sundays preparing for it. We don't need to disappoint our families and friends because the only energy we have for them is what's left over after work takes its share.

We don't need to dress up in suits and business masks, pretending and performing and dreading the thing that should fulfill us. It's not necessary, and it's not good. There are other ways to build our lives and organizations, if only we are brave enough to try.

The debate around what role work should serve in our lives is complex. On the one hand, you might hear, "Love what you do, and you'll never work a day in your life," and in the next moment, "Work is called work for a reason." It can be dizzying, and you might find yourself asking these questions:

- Did I choose the wrong job or career if I'm not having a good time at work?

- Doesn't anything worth doing require struggle and sacrifice?
- Is it my responsibility to make sure my team is enjoying their work? Or is paying them enough?
- Aren't I supposed to be striving for meaning and purpose rather than fun? Didn't fun go the way of the start-up ping pong table a decade ago?
- Okay, sometimes work is fun, but why am I filled with dread every Sunday night?

If one or more of those questions resonated, I see you. I also see a very simple truth, best articulated by the author Annie Dillard: "How we spend our days is, of course, how we spend our lives."

And with that truth, I come down on the side of fun. If I spend roughly one-third of my life at work, I'd like that slice of my pie to be a good one. I want more than meaning, which is certainly important. I also want to be having fun.

This hit me many years ago when I went to visit my mom at an in-patient rehabilitation center after she had a complex ankle surgery. Although my mom was in her early sixties at the time, she was on the spring chicken end of the clientele. To keep morale high, the clinic staff would gather the patients for music performances, and on the day I was there, they had a lovely crooner reprising old Sinatra classics. After a rendition of "My Way," the singer stopped for a bit of stand-up philosophy: "What more could you want, looking back on life, than to have had some good laughs with good people?" I looked around at all the glowing smiles and nodding heads, and it nearly made me weep. All these people knew this truth!

Good laughs with good people . . .

But at the time, good laughs with good people was not what I was prioritizing. I was prioritizing good impact with good metrics. Not to mention good promotion opportunities with good pay. Incidentally, I did have some good days at work, and sure, I liked my colleagues. But that was all secondary.

No longer. Let me be clear about my new point of view, because I recognize it's not conventional wisdom:

All I want is to spend my days with funny, creative, inspiring people who are lovely to hang around. And while we're hanging out, a fun thing to do is create value for others and money for ourselves.

I am not optimizing my impact. (Though that doesn't mean we don't make profound impact.)

I am not optimizing my income. (Though that doesn't mean I'm not making a good income.)

I am not optimizing my growth. (Though that doesn't mean I'm not learning daily.)

I am not even optimizing the meaning of my work. (Though that doesn't mean I don't feel it.)

I am optimizing *good laughs with good people*. Full stop. Because that's what I believe matters in the end, and I'm not afraid to want it.

If this sounds like my teams just sit around chomping bubble gum and shooting darts, I can assure you we only do that on Tuesdays.

As we'll explore together in the coming chapters, perhaps what I'm proudest of in my professional career is my ability to create cozy, supportive, *and* high-performing teams. Because the good people I like hanging around include our clients, and I genuinely care about them. And because there's nothing about having a joyful team that detracts from doing brilliant work! Just the opposite.

"But wait, Bree, are you telling me that I'd be better off if I could get rid of the work part of work and just hang out all day long?" Well, maybe that would float some people's boats, and maybe it'll do it for me in retirement, but at this moment in my life, mid-career, and for many others I suspect, I'd say: no. Because I believe work is fundamentally good.

Work is a nice way to spend our time with each other on this planet. It can be a source of the good laughs, not just bad backs and screen-fatigued eyes. It's fun to build skills. It's fun to make things that help other people. It's fun to make money!

In this chapter we'll wander around why that's true. Why it's possible for most work, most days to be fun, what it looks like, and how you can make it ever more true for yourself.

Here we go!

IN THIS CHAPTER

WORK IS GOOD

Work = force × distance
....

What shall we do while we're here?
....

The desire to work is innate
....

The desire for a trampoline
at work is also innate
....

Work is not fundamentally painful
....

Are you having a good time?
....

Not all days will be fun
....

Resisting the business case for joy
....

Not everyone is burned out
....

Your impact is enough
....

TGIM is possible
....

Work can be better than sex
....

Bank the joy now
....

HOW TO HAVE FUN

Know if your job is even funable
....

Know what you can control
....

Spot and multiply your joy
....

Thin slice your joy
....

WORK IS GOOD

Work = force × distance

Since this is a book about work, perhaps it would be helpful to define it. Take a second and think about your definition.

My mind goes in many directions: Paid labor? Though certainly unpaid labor is still work. I also think of the French word for work: *travail*. The English word, travail, translates to "painful or laborious effort." Oof.

And then I think back to when I was 24 and living in Pasadena teaching high school physics. I remember teaching a simple—and my favorite—definition:

Work = force × distance

I like it because it's straightforward and judgment free. It's just some effort that makes a difference. No more, no less. Which means we get to invent all the rest!

What shall we do while we're here?

There was a time not too long after my mom's cancer diagnosis when, per my mom's wishes, I'd moved my parents from Chicago and finally had them all set up in New York. They had an apartment, doctors, and their finances in order. The whirlwind of the news and the move had died down. I remember sitting in their apartment, knowing the time with my mom was finite, and no longer feeling tied up in time-sensitive to-dos.

I thought to myself, "Well, what shall we do while we're here?"

Which is also the grander question humans have asked themselves over the course of our existence, and the question every human must answer after meeting their basic needs of food and shelter. What parts of life should we try to make better for each other? Whether it be fashion or medicine or coffee bean harvesting, it's all in service of having a better time on this planet while we're here. To improve others' experience as well as our own should feel great.

That is our life's work.

The desire to work is innate

Brad, Arden, and I were sitting in the Who'd A Thought It pub in Lockeridge, England. We had "lived" in this gorgeous little village during the pandemic for four months after our lease was up in NYC. Three years later we were back visiting, enjoying our bangers and mash in the pub. Arden (who was eight at the time) looked over to the bar to see our friend Lauren pouring drinks. Arden whispered to me, "I wish I could do that! I could serve drinks!" She didn't mean one day. She meant like right then. She wanted Lauren's job. And because I was two ciders in, I was like, "That does look fun!" and I kind of wanted Lauren's job, too.

I think it looked fun to Arden because she knows how to pour beer without too much head, and she wanted to show off her skill (I'm hoping Child Protective Services finds this adorable—I swear she doesn't drink it). I think it looked fun because everyone smiled at Lauren when she came around with their drinks. And I think it looked fun when she compared it to the alternative of chatting with her parents.

Children have such an incredible "Can I try?!" muscle that often atrophies over the years when we tell them, "It's faster if I do it... when you're older... I don't have time for a mess..." And then we grow into adults in workplaces where managers say, "It's faster if I do it... when you're more senior... we won't have time to redo it..."

But the instinct to work is always there, however muted, because it is fundamentally alluring. We want to show off our skills, to have people thank us, to do something other than sit around.

I hope you feel that "Can I try?" urge once in a while. It's your inner child, just wanting to pour the beer.

The desire for a trampoline at work is also innate

I'm sitting next to Arden while we wait for her swim team practice to start. Having just written about our innate and childlike desire for work, I figure I'll ask her what she thinks the best part of having a job will be. I brace myself for the brilliant, uncommon wisdom only a child can impart.

She says, "What job would it be? Working at a trampoline park? Then the best part would be jumping on the trampoline."

Obviously.

Work is not fundamentally painful

You don't get paid because work is painful and people wouldn't do it otherwise. You get paid because you create value. The pain is entirely optional!

At the beginning of my work life, when I was teaching seventh grade math in Pasadena, I remember thinking to myself, "I hope they don't realize I'd do this job for free!" Of course I needed to pay my bills, so an income was necessary. But in a world where I had been conditioned to believe payment for work is because work is painful, I felt like I was cheating the system.

Work is simply making or doing things that others appreciate—effort that makes a difference. And that is fun! It's all the other cluttery stuff we put around work (approval processes! aimless meetings! suits!) that makes it dreadful. When we strip away all that stuff that clutters up work, we find something lovely: something we can give ourselves to that gives back to us in equal measure.

Dart Lindsley, host of the podcast *Work for Humans*, has a beautiful way to think about the value you get from your job. He's pioneering the idea that work is not only an input to the value a company creates but also a product in and of itself. He's famous for asking his podcast guests (and probably most people he meets) this question:

What job do you "hire" your job to do for you?

Some people hire their job to teach them skills or to give them puzzles or to provide an audience. I hire my job to provide me with the good people with whom I have good laughs.

Michael: All he does is work.

Buddy the Elf: But work is fun!

Michael: Not the way he does it…

Are you having a good time?

Sometimes it helps me to zoom out so I can see the big picture. Not as in, "What am I doing with my life?" but way, way out, as in, "What are we Earthlings doing with our existence?"

In these uber-existential moments, I imagine a giant cosmic light switch that ends life on Earth forever. Imagining we had the opportunity for a little Earth post-mortem, what would we make of humans' existence? What would be the ultimate metric of success?

We could consider productivity and how much we accomplished, or more poetic things like how much we helped each other. But I think it boils down to this:

"Did we have a good time?"

This isn't a call for empty hedonism. It's a call to start valuing our own experiences—something businesses too easily discard. I've read about one million articles about the business case for culture and employee experience. It's all true, but it's also not the point. Those employees experiencing that employee experience? That's just us! WE are the employees, all the way from the front line to leadership. That experience is the lives we're living—our finite days on the planet!—not an input to productivity. Shouldn't we value that experience more? Shouldn't we be enjoying ourselves?

One winter we traveled through the Scottish Highlands, and we stayed at a small inn that hosted all the guests at a communal dinner. I sat next to a lovely woman, and as dinner progressed and whisky flowed, the conversation moved from the weather to dead parents (as it is wont to do). She had lost her mother the prior year at the beautiful age of 95. After her mother passed, she and her siblings found a note their mother had left with instructions for her funeral. Songs, flowers, and the like. At the bottom of the note was this single sentence:

"I had a great time!"

As tears streamed down my face listening to this story (I dare say I would have cried even without the whisky), I thought to myself, "That's it! That's all there is, and it's everything." Just as you would say leaving a party with friends (not a bad metaphor for life, btw), what more could you ask to say as you leave life?

One of the thoughts that helped me most when processing my own mom's death is imagining her on a Ferris wheel. Instead of being angry that her last few decades were taken from her, I just imagine that her ride was 73 years long. She went up and around and when the time came, she got off the ride. I know in my bones she had a great time.

Not all days will be fun

I'm a fan of the word "most," as in "Most work, most days, should be fun." I'm an optimist, but I'm not unrealistic. Some work just isn't enjoyable, for whatever reason. I don't love making slide decks and I've spent ages in consulting anyway. Some days you tried your hardest and still you fail in ways big or small. Or someone gets upset about something you did. But you don't need me to tell you that some days at work are bad. In those moments, it's fine to not be having any fun.

There's an old Norwegian response to "How are you?" that you might find relevant on these days:

Oppe og ikke gråter.

It means "up and not crying."

On a not-that-fun kind of day, up and not crying is plenty.

Resisting the business case for joy

I am not going to make the business case for joy even though there is a massive one for it. Just look at organizations such as Starbucks and Pfizer, which both have joy as one of their few values. It's in the corporate lexicon and elevated to the highest levels of how businesses define themselves for good reason. It's good for business—yes. But I'm tired of making the business case for human things. Let companies make the human case for business things!

For example, as well-intentioned as the argument is, if I hear one more time that rest is good for productivity, I'm going to throw that person's egg timer out the window. Sure, yes, but FAR more important is that rest is good for enjoying your life! It's good for having a healthy body that will carry you as long as possible. Rest is good because, well, it's just fucking nice to wake up after a nap. That's what rest is good for. And as much as I care about your business (and I take supporting leadership and business seriously), I care *more* about if you're enjoying your life. If you're happy. And for the love of all things good—if you're rested.

In other words, rest is about *savoring* the world, not gearing up to *save* the world on Monday.

So next time you're tempted to do weekend work but your body needs a nap: nap. If it's noon on a workday but nothing is pressing and you're debating answering another email or enjoying a sunny walk around the block: walk. If you see your parent or partner or friend's name pop up on your phone but answering it would mean pausing work: answer that call. Otherwise, the moment will pass you by, and the joy you might have had will go with it.

Not everyone is burned out

MONICA: *You don't even like your job.*
CHANDLER: *So? Who does?*
PHOEBE: *Oh I like my job!*
JOEY: *I love my job.*
RACHEL: *I can't wait to go back to work.*
ROSS: *I can't get enough dinosaurs!*

I was facilitating an executive leadership team gathering recently, and we were discussing culture and burnout. One leader said, "But at what company *isn't* there burnout?" I looked around the room and saw most people nodding their heads. Sometimes we find ourselves as Chandler, assuming that because we don't particularly like our jobs or we feel burned out, that's the state of work for everyone. But then you meet someone like Ross who CAN'T GET ENOUGH DINOSAURS and think, "Huh, that's possible? Then why isn't it true for me?"

To be clear, I never want to make anyone feel bad or ashamed about not having fun at work. I simply want to de-normalize the notion that "Nobody likes work and everyone is exhausted." Because when we normalize a fun-less state of work, we lose the belief that it's even *possible* for things to be different. We tell ourselves stories that sound like:

- "Work is stressful . . . that's why they pay me the big bucks!" (Recall: they pay you the big bucks because you create value. The pain is entirely optional.)
- "Everyone is burned out, and I don't even have it as bad as [zombie-eyed colleague]."
- "I'm not an hourly worker. Working nights and weekends is just part of being a full-time, salaried employee."

Rough days and even rough months are normal, and we endure, but I don't want anyone to endure rough years before they decide to make a change. Because if there's a better job and life set-up out there, I want us all to spend as many of our precious days in it as possible.

Your impact is enough

We get very mixed messages about what makes a good job. It should be deeply meaningful and become your legacy. It should use all your skills. It should pay well and be prestigious and carry an impressive title. And did you remember to scale your impact, preferably at the million- or billion-person scale? Are you a Very Important Person? Are you making your dent in the universe?

For fuck's sake! That sounds exhausting.

Let me tell you a story I used to love but now I hate. I used to open presentations to leadership teams with it and tell it proudly. And then one day when I was thinking of incorporating it into a presentation, I thought to myself, "What am I saying? I don't believe in this!"

The story goes that in 1962, President JFK was visiting NASA. During his visit, he walked by a janitor in the hallway. He took the occasion to introduce himself: "Hi, I'm Jack Kennedy. What are you doing there?" The janitor responded, "Well, Mr. President, I'm helping to put a man on the moon."

I used to tell the story to showcase the impact of purpose: how every role in an organization, large and small, should feel a connection to, and ability to contribute to, the purpose of the company. Whenever I've told the story, people have responded with awe, and I get it—there's much to be said about being a part of something bigger than yourself. And no one dares question the value of scale in organizations today: Reach more customers! Make more impact! Change the world!

Here's my rebuttal, and it might not be popular:

Valuing scale as the ultimate aim is what turns us from humans into human resources.

When you value world-changing scale as the ultimate awe-worthy goal, you simultaneously devalue human-scaled, one-on-one impact.

The janitor could have responded, "I'm taking care of this floor, in this building, in this corner of the world because it's important. I'm making life a bit cleaner and easier and happier for Anne in engineering and Joe in communications." That doesn't have the same awe-factor, does it? But I'd argue that it should because taking care of each other on a human scale is important. It's important to Anne and Joe. Isn't it enough to know he's making their lives better without needing to change the course of humanity?

Let me go further.

Valuing world-scale over human-scale is also biased. In this narrative of "impact at scale," do you know who sleeps best at night? CEOs. Presidents. Executive directors. Everyone else has to engage in mental gymnastics to connect clean floors to a milestone of humanity.

"Impact at scale" is also one of capitalism's favorite anthems. When organizations can get their people to all sing the song of scale, business grows. But that same song also devalues the one-on-one, human-centered professions like nursing and teaching that people say are so important but, at least in the US, aren't paid as such. A teacher doesn't scale. A kindergarten teacher reaches maybe 30 kids a year. Over a 40-year career, that's 1,200 students, which sounds like a lot until you start humming the song of scale. Does the teacher need to believe they're raising a generation, or is it enough to look at the student in front of them and see growth and passion and pride and happiness? Which has made a more positive, lasting impact on your life: Your favorite teacher? Or the textbook you used in that class that scaled to millions of other students? Although scale is the dream of many businesses, it's not the lever that often creates real impact.

Despite sounding grumpy, I mean this as a hopeful notion. You don't need to bend the arc of the universe for your work to be meaningful. Your work can be meaningful because you've made Anne's and Joe's lives a little better. Your joy matters. The joy you create matters. You can enjoy that they say hello, that they smile as they see you cleaning the floors. You don't have to believe, "I'm helping put a man on the moon." You can simply say, "I'm making life better right here, for people I know and care about, on Earth."

And that is enough.

TGIM is possible

Back when I was teaching, Friday afternoons were oddly hard. I don't know if it was the kids or the sense of responsibility or the palm trees all around the school, but I do know that when I drove home, I felt a come-down from all the fun I had that week. I was disappointed that I'd have to wait until Monday to tell more stupid jokes about fractions to make a classroom of 12-year-olds groan-smile. On Friday afternoons, I felt like a kid at an amusement park getting off a ride, shouting, "Again! Again!"

I feel that way after the last executive leaves an offsite I facilitate and the team can finally shout, "We did it!" and bask in the glow of the positive feedback. It's not every day I feel this way, but it's enough for me to know I love this ride, and most weeks I'm excited to go again.

What makes you shout, "Again! Again!"? How can you pull more of that into your work and life so you can say, "Thank god it's Monday"?

Work can be better than sex

Allow me to introduce you to someone who shouted "Again! Again!" his whole life through. His name is Milton Glaser, and he was one of the greatest designers to ever live.

He was born in 1929 and died in 2020 at age 91. He's had one-man shows at the Museum of Modern Art and the Centre Pompidou. He was selected for lifetime achievement awards by the Cooper Hewitt, Smithsonian Design Museum and the Fulbright Association. He was the first graphic designer to receive the National Medal of Arts award, which he received from former President Obama. Famously, he is the designer behind I ♥ NY and he co-founded *New York Magazine*.

My colleague and dear friend Sue Walsh worked as Milton's senior art director for almost a decade. Through Sue's stories I have fallen completely in love with this genius who so desperately loved work and life. I think you might, too. Sue kindly agreed to let me interview her about her time working with Milton, and you'll see our conversation pop up throughout the book. Like our own little Yoda, Milton will visit us, whispering wisdom about work, life, and pasta alle vongole.

The first thing you should know about Milton is that he had fun at work. Like maybe the *most* fun. Sue told me he would begin each day by saying, "Let's have a good time." When asked in an interview for the *New York Times* why he kept working at age 87, he smiled and said:

You really want an answer? It's the greatest source of pleasure in my life. I am so thrilled by making something that didn't exist before... I also think there's an opportunity to do good. Not in a moralistic sense, but to feel that you're a part of something larger than yourself. But that's not really why I do it. I do it because it is so pleasurable for me. I derive this deep, deep satisfaction that nothing else, including sex, has ever given me.

You heard it here first, folks: *work is better than sex.*

Perhaps you can debate that in the Amazon reviews of this book one day. What I love about Milton's response is that it's so honest. He flirts for a hot second with the "right" answer to the interview question: "I work to create positive impact" (which I don't doubt is part of it). But ultimately lands on what work really is to him: FUN.

Bank the joy now

I like the word "fun" because it's so visceral and pure. At any given moment, you can usually tell if you're having fun (and you can *always* tell if you're *not* having fun). I think of "joy" as a more reflective feeling, one that encompasses poignancy, beauty, and gratitude. I sometimes use them interchangeably in this book, and honestly, you can pick your favorite.

But, contrary to popular opinion, I specifically do *not* like holding up "meaning" or "purpose" as our ultimate aims. They're good things, to be sure, but I also think they're dangerous within a prevailing culture of overwork. Why? Because those words, "meaning" and "purpose," have a sneaky way of disguising a dreadful and intense working experience as a struggle for excellence and what is needed to build a legacy. In other words, work may not be fun, but it will be worth it.

Maybe.

Sometimes.

If you're genuinely happy working intensely, then far be it from me to object. But too many people are not. Or perhaps they tell themselves they are because they don't see another way.

I recognize "sacrifice now for reward later" is generally a good principle when it comes to health and wealth (Are you maxing out your IRAs?). But it can easily be taken too far by the religion of workism—it's sneaky like that! It's up to us to consider: For what cost now? And for what reward?

It might help to ask yourself:

Did I choose for work to be this hard/intense/unpleasant, or did my company choose it for me? Do you want it? And if you do, why? Is this working experience what you intended for yourself?

Am I clear-eyed about the price? Is the struggle worth an early heart attack one day? Is it worth the sleep deprivation? The toll on your mental health? What about the others in your life? What price do they pay? As one Redditor said, "20 years from now, the only people who will remember that you worked late are your kids."

Is it the right choice for my life now? We all have seasons of life, and some may be good for digging in, but is that time now?

Do I believe the intensity will be worth it in the end? And by end, I do mean the *end*. The Stoic evangelist Ryan Holiday writes, "The Roman poet Juvenal joked that while Alexander was living, the whole world could not contain him, but in death a coffin was sufficient. The humbling wisdom of the joke is one we ought to remember too as we save 'for retirement,' as we 'invest for the future,' as we 'build our legacy.' It's very cheap to be dead."

There's a lot of pressure to bank the hard work and paychecks now. And of course, hard work and paychecks are excellent things. They're just not the *only* things worth banking.

Bank the joy now. Bank the smiles of people whose lives you make better. Bank the pride you feel for doing a good job. And when you get home, bank the good times with your family and friends. Bank your health. Your rest. A memory. You won't get to enjoy your posthumous fame and fortune. That's why, starting today, I invite you to start making work fun.

Most days, anyway.

HOW TO HAVE FUN

Know if your job is even funable

If you're not having any fun, the first question is whether your current role and company are funable in the first place.

Most of this section will be about finding more fun and joy in your current situation, but I don't want to skip the fact that some jobs or life set-ups are just not a good fit.

Sometimes the fit isn't good because there is an evident toxic work culture. Sometimes the demands of the role are more than you're willing to invest. Sometimes the job is too easy and there's no growth. And sometimes it's a wonderful role at a wonderful company that you've simply outgrown. I fully understand it's not always possible to quit, but I also know there are many times when it is, and we don't.

How do you know when you should quit? Some people will say you should spend at least *x* years at a company. Others will say to leave if you can find a *z* percent higher salary elsewhere. But I subscribe to author Cheryl Strayed's philosophy of when to leave relationships. It applies just as well to jobs. If your very truest, most honest voice inside yourself says go, then go. In her words:

Go, even though there is nowhere to go.
Go, even though you don't know exactly why you can't stay.
Go, because you want to.
Because wanting to leave is enough.

Now back to reality. Ideally you have one of those six-month emergency funds financial advisors are always going on about or another role lined up if you can't afford a gap. If you're looking for more fun, unemployment definitely isn't it. But the sentiment remains: you don't need a fancy, well-reasoned argument for leaving a role. If in your gut you want to go, it's time to go. Every day you spend in a role that isn't working for you is one of your precious and finite days on this planet. Eventually, you will run out, no two ways about it.

Kind of a bummer way to start a section about fun, huh?

Don't worry, it gets better. A few chapters from now we'll talk about losing your life's work!

Perhaps you're now wondering if I ever get invited to parties. I do, really...

Know what you can control

You may recognize the serenity prayer popularized by Alcoholics Anonymous:

God, grant me the serenity to accept the things I cannot change, the courage to change the things I can, and the wisdom to know the difference.

Surprising to some, it's not from an ancient religious text. Some unknown person around 1930 just thought it made sense and wrote it down. But the notion was around long before and comprises the core of Stoic philosophy from 300 BC.

As it relates to us, it's very simple. Everything pertaining to your work and whether you're having fun can be divided into two categories:

1 Things you can control.
2 Things you can't control.

As the prayer says, the trick is in not confusing the two.

You are not going to work— you are going to have fun.

BÉLA FRANCIA to his wife, Nobel Prize–winner Katalin Karikó, whose work in mRNA led to the development of the COVID vaccines

Spot and multiply your joy

Let's dive into what we *can* control. We have so many levers to make our work lives more fun! Below is an exercise I invite you to do with your team that is designed to help you spot and multiply your joy.

Recall: Ask your team to think back over the last three to six months and individually identify and jot down a moment when they were having the most fun. You should do this, too.

If it's been a rough few months, even a simple, "I just really liked that moment!" is good enough. If your last few months have been great ones, then you might think back to when you felt the most eroticism at work.

Sorry, if you work in HR and need a minute to finish reading that last sentence, take your time. If you're having an office affair and are wondering how I knew—gotcha! Just kidding. Here we'll use psychotherapist Esther Perel's definition of eroticism: "The qualities of vitality, curiosity, and spontaneity that make us feel alive." Have you ever felt like that at work?

Categorize: Before sharing, ask your team to identify the joy at the heart of their selected moment (you can pick more than one):

- ☐ Joy in the **making**
- ☐ Joy in the **people**
- ☐ Joy in using your **skills**
- ☐ Joy in **adventure**
- ☐ Joy in the **product**
- ☐ Joy in what else?

Share: As a team, share your answers in a round, both the moment and the source of joy.

Discuss: Did anyone have the same moment? What made that moment so impactful? Even among different moments, were there patterns or commonalities in the sources of joy?

Brainstorm: As a team, decide which sources of joy you want more of. For those categories, read the descriptions below aloud and brainstorm what you might do together.

Pro tip: Focus on the strengths of your situation and look for even more joy there, rather than on shoring up un-funness.

Pro-but-I'm-not-totally-ready-for-this tip: If you can't imagine gathering a team for this feel-y of an exercise, start by doing it yourself and see what comes.

Joy in the making

How can you protect more heads-down time for everyone to focus on making? Or if needed, how can you protect more focused team working time for collaboration? Could one person on the team be on call for any emails/requests of the team for that time so the rest of the team can focus?

For example, tasked with creating a captivating experience for our client's customers, we took ourselves on a "Do Nothing Day" in which we took no meetings, emailed no emails, and just sat with each other in the park dreaming. About 80 percent of the ideas we ended up executing came from this day of "nothingness." (More on Do Nothing Days in chapter 4.)

Joy in the people on the team

How can you spend more time together? If you're a distributed team, could one person teach the rest of the team a skill (e.g., knot tying, calligraphy) over Zoom?

If you're able to work in person, can you align your days in the office (or a coffee shop) to jam together and maybe share a meal?

How can you ensure you're checking in with each other at the top of the day as humans, before you take on what the day has in store for you? (A daily check-in works great for this! Instructions for check-ins will come in chapter 3.)

For example, during the pandemic, our team made time for a virtual pasta making class, led by our teammate Sasha, who went to culinary school before she turned to design.

Joy in using your skills

I'm all for learning and growth, but also, sometimes it's exhausting!

How can you help team members "play in position" so they can showcase the best of their strengths? Can you host a monthly show-and-tell at which team members can showcase a skill they have (e.g., a strategy for writing code or a research technique) and teach others? Can you experiment with a new division of labor within the team so that everyone is playing to their strengths?

For example, I once gave an internal presentation to my colleagues about public speaking. In it, I shared my best tricks for what to do with your body and voice on a stage (all learned from my speaking coach, the luminary Nick Morgan). For months and now years after that presentation, people still bring up "toaster arms" in conversation (the idea that you don't want closed body language on stage—better to have your arms out and open, as if you're a piece of bread in a toaster not wanting to get burned). It was such a small presentation, but I felt so proud and had so much fun that it stands out as a bright spot in my career.

Joy in adventure

How can you revel in the war stories you're collecting today?

One of the great silver linings of hard times is that they often make for great stories later. I never tell the story about the flight I took that was perfectly on time. But I've often told the story about getting stranded in Toronto after 16 hours of travel. I found myself crying in the terminal, and the kind customs agent invited me to stay with her for the night and have dinner with her family. I accepted!

I also never tell the story of my last project going as planned. Instead, I tell the story of our team working in the lobby of a Seattle hotel late into the night wearing bathrobes (we had pajamas underneath; don't worry, no eroticism here). We were pushing to finish the design of an organization-wide experience to be presented the next day. We'd received all sorts of helpful feedback earlier that day from the client but had only one night to revise. As you know by now, I think chronic (or even semi-frequent) over-work is unhealthy and unfun and un-lots of other things. But once in a blue moon when conditions are right, it's invigorating to dive in with abandon.

Anyway, when you're exhausted and at the end of your rope, just remember, you're going to really impress someone at a cocktail party one day.

Joy in the product

How can you amplify the pride you feel in your product-baby and its impact? Can you share it with others in the organization? Can you refer back to your first version and enjoy how far you've come? Can you take time to just look at it and be happy?

I'll be honest, sometimes I'm so excited about a metaphor or a turn of phrase that I'll just read it over and over feeling pleased with myself. Self-indulgent? Perhaps, but I don't care one bit. It feels good to applaud yourself!

Within the design world, "crit" sessions are prevalent as opportunities for others to critique your work to make it stronger. But once you're done with those, maybe you hold a "fawn" session and invite people—or even just the team that made it—to comment on all the things they love about it and the impact it made. Why the hell not?

Thin slice your joy

Maybe you're like, "Nope, Bree, I tried and I'm still not having fun. What do you have for me?"

Well wouldn't you know it, I have some robust experience with "this is complete shit" situations, so I have a trick up my sleeve. Let's start with what is categorically *not* fun: worrying constantly about your mother with stage 4 cancer. Don't get me wrong, we had some great fun together during her last months, but there were many, many moments when I felt completely obliterated.

This was my best trick to overcoming that obliteration: when the big, difficult things felt too big and difficult, I "thin sliced" my joy.

I remember sitting in a taxi as it wound its way through Central Park. I was on my way to the hospital to visit my mom. It was February and (it shocks me every year) the daffodils were already emerging from their slumber. They were so beautiful, and it gave me this "ooh, it's coming!" feeling I've always enjoyed about each season's approach.

Trying to comprehend an unimaginable diagnosis will always feel debilitating. But you know what's kind of okay? This minute.

Even when life wasn't okay, that small minute was just fine. My mom was okay at that minute, probably having her breakfast. I was okay. Nothing hurt.

Thin slicing your joy can show up in different ways.

Does this month at work feel worrisome and stressful? Well maybe this day is okay as you make progress.

This day feels too much? Maybe this one hour in this one meeting feels manageable.

This hour feels like days? Try living just in this minute, next to the daffodils.

When I need to pull out all the stops, I follow author Cheryl Strayed's guidance: "You can mark your progress breath by breath."

Thin slicing may look like getting yourself a cappuccino with cinnamon on top to take with you into a hard conversation. Amidst the stress, you can take a breath, smell the cinnamon, and take a sip. Or maybe your entire project is going south so you schedule a one-on-one with a colleague you trust so you can thoroughly complain about it. In doing so you build trust and friendship. Remember, even soldiers on the front lines play poker sometimes.

When the picture of your work or life looks like chaos, trust that you can always find a pixel of peace.

Closing thought

The ultimate question, in song form.
Step 1: Get yourself a delightful snack.
Step 2: Go here and press play.
Step 3: Enjoy!

2

YOUR BRAIN WORKS WHETHER YOU'RE WEARING A SUIT OR STRETCHY PANTS

What am I wearing right now, you ask? How very cheeky of you. If you must know, I'm wearing sweatpants, a button-down flannel shirt, and my puffer coat because it's chilly in this café. My hair is mostly wet since I exercised this morning, showered, and, you know, misplaced all my fucks and didn't have a single one to give to dolling myself up.

Science tells us what makes the brain work well: good sleep, good nutrition, good exercise, good mental health. Funny how those four things are often the first to be sacrificed to a busy workday. We say things like, "What's keeping you up at night?" when asking people about their work concerns. We down caffeine as liquid energy, forgo exercise because we're too zonked after a day of meetings, and then refuse to unplug.

Athletes treat their bodies impeccably with finely tuned nutrition and training schedules. A world-class musician practices and plays only the finest instrument and has it cared for by the most skilled artisans. But knowledge workers? Brain athletes, if you will? We eagerly trash our brains if it means getting more done, regardless of the quality.

Before Arden was born, Brad and I looked for a financial advisor to help us get our house in order. We interviewed one man in a suit who proudly touted, "Don't worry—I never sleep! I'm working seven days a week and up at 5 am, so I'm here for whatever you need." I appreciated that he wanted to be seen as available, but my first thought was whether I wanted a harried, overworked, sleep-deprived person giving us advice on our life savings. I don't care if someone looks the part or meets society's standards for hustle culture. I want the expert whose brain works best. (I'll write much more on this in the chapter about brilliant work.)

Somewhere along the way we have decided to equate smart and professional with well-dressed and well-groomed, rather than well-exercised, well-rested, well-fed, and happy. We've confused *being* professional with *looking* professional.

What is professional	What looks professional
Being respectful of others' time	Fancy tailored clothes
Being just plain respectful	Exceptional personal grooming
Keeping your cool in hard moments	A thousand unfortunate biases, including being tall, "broad shouldered," old enough to look wise, but not too old to be out of touch, serious, not to mention rich, white, and male
Being prepared	
Delivering high-quality work	
Being reliable and responsive	
	Glasses always help, and maybe throw in a British accent

It's silly. Can we all decide the new professionalism means being rested and happy and respectful and *actually* good at our work, WHETHER OR NOT we're wearing a zipper?

Also, it's really no fun. Who wants to be (literally) buttoned up and proper all day long? Why should work be a costume party? If work should be fun, then the first thing we have to let go of is needing to be super profesh.

IN THIS CHAPTER

Your brain works whether you're wearing a suit or stretchy pants

PROFESSIONALISM IS A BUZZKILL

Work is performative

Your Michelin-starred meal is a bunch of dead plants and animals. Your marble countertops are old rock. And your fitted suit is sheep hair sewn into a business costume.

Work is in many ways performative, and I understand why. No one really knows what they're doing, and yet our ability to get things done rests on other people believing that we do. So we've created symbols of professionalism that we use to telegraph competency.

We wear tailored suits so we look like what society tells us businesspeople look like. We use buzzwords and jargon to obscure our lack of clear thinking. And we banter about being in "back-to-back" meetings because that's how in-demand professionals spend their days.

But we need exactly none of it. No suits, no buzzwords, no banter, no performance. Your brain works whether you're wearing a suit or stretchy pants. And that's great! Because stretchy pants are fantastic.

Costumes are unnecessary

I'm sitting in the lobby of a Hyatt in Chicago with two colleagues. We're preparing for a pitch at a client's office in a few hours. One colleague, Sarah, feels like an old friend. We've worked closely together before, and she's one of those people who makes me more confident just being in her presence. The other, Pla, feels like a new friend. She's someone

I don't know well but feel instantly comfortable around. I'm in a T-shirt and stretch joggers, sitting cross-legged. We laugh as we work, and then the meeting time approaches. "Time to get our costumes on!" Sarah says. And we all head up to our rooms to don our blazers and pressed pants.

It was nice while it lasted.

Professionalism dulls

Remember Milton Glaser from chapter 1? The man who said work was better than sex? In my interview with Sue, his long-time associate, she shared that Milton also had some thoughts about professionalism.

....

Sue: Milton never wanted to be a professional. That was one of his parting words when I moved on from his studio; he was like, "Don't get too professional." I clearly still think about that many years later.

Me: What do you think he meant, or what does it mean to you to "not get too professional"?

Sue: Just don't get molded into another form of being in the world as a designer, where you're going to meet the objectives and deliver what you are told to deliver and do the things you're asked to do in the right way, and not still retain this integrity and imagination and capacity for new thinking. Professionalism meant, for Milton, moving too far from the life of an artist and too close to the life of a businessperson. Designers exist in the middle of that spectrum.

....

That's what the business costume does to us: it molds us into a cog in the machine. Not to mention it's a little pinchy around the waist and our imaginations.

Conformity is the enemy of inclusion

It's not that I'm opposed to fashion. I mean, I'm not particularly fashionable myself (and my daughter will eagerly tell you that), though I appreciate that some people's favorite mode of creative expression happens to be wearable. But that's not what we're talking about here—not really. We're talking about conformity.

Back in the early days of Facebook, Mark Zuckerberg popularized the business hoodie. Regardless of your feelings about him today, he was right about one thing: a suit does not make you better at business. And in fact, openly rebelling against "business as usual" in dress is a way to rebel against it in function as well, which invites a culture of upending the status quo. The fashion platform Betabrand picked up on this and started making "Dress Pant Yoga Pants" and the "Executive Pinstripe Hoodie" to make fun of the absurdity of the business costume.

But the business costume is more than absurd. It does real harm in the workplace.

When expected to dress a certain way for work, many people in marginal-ized communities don't feel complete in their business outfit without their business mask. That mask is the way of speaking and acting that matches the dominant culture. It means actively trying to figure out how to fit in and then working really fucking hard to do it—not just because inclusion feels nice, but because your job may be at risk if you don't. The busi-ness mask also obscures the fact that you have responsibilities or needs outside work, as if everyone has a stay-at-home wife who is handling all domestic tasks and caregiving (including for you) so you can devote long hours to the business.

The business costume kills psychological safety, inclusion, and any sense of humanity or true camaraderie. It's exhausting for those who have to pretend, and it simultaneously mutes the vibrancy, creativity, and talents they might otherwise have contributed.

Interviewer: Do you think of yourself as a style icon?

Jerry Seinfeld: No. Are you kidding? I just want to be comfortable and get out of the goddamn house.

Consider these quotes from research I did with one financial services client years ago. They were proud of their professionalism—especially given the stakes of their industry—but their brand of professionalism only bred conformity:

- "There's a way of speaking, and others who have a colorful personality or speak differently struggle to fit in."
- "We have a great culture if you know how to fill in the prescription. If you're on the outside, it's hard. People do not invest in them."
- "The feedback was focused on delivery, not content. We've gotten better but have work to do around embracing people, their styles."
- "There shouldn't be one template of what a successful leader is."

Business conformity is harmful for those who must pretend. It's harmful for the business. It's harmful for society. And that's why we need a stretchy pants revolution.

Difference versus defect

Imagine a leader giving a junior colleague the cringey feedback that they need to dress more like this or speak more like that. I myself once received the feedback that I was too bubbly for an executive audience. It's a hard balance, because we don't live in an unbiased world, and we want ourselves and others to succeed in it.

I almost wrote an article called "Sales for Ladies" about everything I had learned about "selling while female." Things like picking the center or head seat at the table and dropping my voice to sound fuller and deeper. I hate that those things have legit helped me, but they have.

Nevertheless, most people want to improve the world while living in it. So before giving anyone else feedback you think might help them, your first question is to ask whether the way someone is doing something is a *defect* or simply a *difference*. Is the way they're dressing or speaking functionally worse, as in does it affect the quality of the work? Or is it simply different from the way it's usually done?

Consider a Boston-based executive leadership team led by a CEO with a Boston accent. Should that CEO give feedback on how to speak properly to their new COO who has a British accent? Of course not! Speaking with a different accent is not a defect; it's just different. It has no bearing on that leader's quality of thought or work.

There's a term for when employees change their voice, language, appearance, and general vibe to fit in with a dominant culture: code switching. It's a burden borne disproportionately by people of color and other historically marginalized communities.

According to a survey from Indeed, around 40 percent of Black workers say that if they stopped code switching, their careers would suffer. LaFawn Davis, chief people and sustainability officer at Indeed, says, "Anytime you can't really be your authentic self, anytime you have to really have it in front of your mind, 'This is who I have to be in this space,' that chips away at a lot, chips away at confidence."

That stinks!

Maybe the best thing we can do as leaders is model non-conformity, in whatever way we can. You can even start with legwear.

The alien test

Meet Bob. He's a friendly, practical alien who comes from an advanced civilization. He's been sent to Earth to observe humanity and figures he'll check out the humans in their habitat of the so-called modern office.

As he makes his rounds, he notices these luxurious strangling devices that humans, in particular male humans, tend to wear when trying to impress other humans. He wonders what function they serve. They look a lot like the leashes that humans put on the dogs they hold prisoner. Maybe male human necks get particularly chilly in the offices they keep at 62 degrees? Interestingly, he notes, these noosed humans seem to always want to loosen these "ties," as they call them, or take them off. And yet they put them on again the next day.

He writes in his report: "Ties: do not recommend."

Back on Earth, in *The New York Times* article "Will the Tie Ever Make a Comeback?" style writer Derek Guy claimed that "the owner of one high-end men's clothing store told him that he 'considers his necktie displays now to be part of the shop's decor, like bars that display antique liquor ads or paper currencies now defunct.'"

HOW TO WORK LIKE A HUMAN

Model humanity

To give you some ideas on how to model humanity in your leadership, here's what I do with my teams:

- I show up to Zoom meetings with sopping wet hair. Because sometimes I exercise, come home, shower, and then jump on a call. I choose having a strong, healthy body over looking like the business world wants me to look. My brain works whether my hair is wet or dry.

- I make and eat lunch during meetings. Because I am a human who needs to eat, and while a better scenario would be having a proper break for lunch, if there's a day when the calendars haven't given me a well-timed break, I'm sure as hell not going to starve myself out of professionalism. It's ridiculous to have to model eating lunch, but I want my team to know that if they're hungry, it's okay for them to eat. Prisoners get their meals on time—why shouldn't office workers?

- I say what's happening in my life outside work. I'm tired because I had to take my dad to the ER yesterday. I'm excited because I got new pajamas and they're killer. I feel self-conscious because my hair is doing this weird flip thing today, but you all don't mind, do you?

- I really do wear stretchy pants. Sometimes it's exercise pants so I can exercise right after work. Sometimes it's exercise pants and I'm not going to exercise after work—they're just good pants! I'll admit when meeting with a client, especially a new client, I'll sometimes wear stretchy black jeans. Hasn't gotten me fired yet!

Risk unprofessionalism

Client: We already have some of that content ourselves, but it's not inspiring.

Me: The good news is we have a body of work to pull from. We can definitely infuse a more modern take throughout and design a new platform for it. Oh, sorry, just one second, I'll be right back. Carrie, do you want to talk about next steps?

Meeting continues.

Me: Okay, I'm back. Yes, that all sounds great. We'll do a draft and share it with you next week!

Meeting ends.

Team gets on another Zoom to debrief the client call.

Me: That was great! And, Carrie, thanks so much for picking up at the end there. I needed to go take a picture of my cat.

Team: . . .

Me: Well, she was all curled up in my daughter's doll stroller. She's never done that before! Felt like something worth prioritizing. I'll put the picture in Slack. You'll agree when you see it.

Tell me it's not worth leaving a meeting for:

Talk like a human

Bob decided to learn English before making his trek to Earth—a widely used business language, he read. While observing a strategic planning meeting, he made a mental note to leave a bad review for his language program, Rosetta Meteor.

"I don't know what I studied, but it is NOT the English these people are speaking. Who owns these ducks they're getting in a row? There are no fruit trees anywhere in this building, let alone low-hanging fruit. And my god I hope they don't try to boil their oceans."

He keeps listening, intent on learning how to "speak business."

In his report he instructs:

To speak business, you must ignore the humans' hoopla about efficiency and clarity. You must instead use the most poofy-sounding words available.

For example, when humans mean "use," they don't say "use," they say "leverage." When they mean "to-do," they say "action item." And want to guess what "user-centered innovation" means? "Make better stuff that people like!"

This was all quite comical until I learned the term for people. "Human resources." Apparently they've declared themselves fuel.

I admire women who look as if they know who they are and are comfortable telegraphing that to the world … Which is, really, the ultimate grown-up way to dress.

VANESSA FRIEDMAN, chief fashion critic for *The New York Times*

Humanize your space

If you've ever been in a hotel conference room as part of an offsite, you'll know the set up: a pad of paper and pen set up next to a glass of water. It's all part of a "Yes, yes, we are doing the business!" message. Ironically, this is how executive teams come together to be creative and brilliantly chart a course for the organization.

I like writing things down and drinking water as much as the next person, but it's the subtext here that just makes me say "WHY?" The subtext is that business is serious and strict and you need these kinds of barren functional tools to do it: pen, paper, water.

You know what I would love to see placed at every seat?

- Fidget toys.
- Gel pens. Or fountain pens! Or glow-in-the-dark pens.
- Tiny bottles of different juices labeled "Creativity!" "Strategic Vision!" and "Calm."
- Ooh, what about blankets on the chairs, like some restaurants have in the winter for their outdoor seating? It's always too hot or too cold in those rooms.
- And maybe happy lamps? Most of those rooms don't have windows, and nobody is their most creative stuck in a white box with artificial lighting for nine hours.
- And it would be REALLY fun to have slippers for everyone, but the room might get smelly if everyone took off their shoes.

If work should be fun, if we don't have to look professional, what would you put in the room? Also, maybe for your next team offsite, do it! What would you want?

Dress for joy

Fiona Harvey, a public health and wellness expert, talks about the concept of "dopamine dressing," or wearing "clothing that makes you feel joyous." For some, this might mean going glam. For me, it's my favorite flannel, because it makes me feel like myself. How cool would it be if you showed up to work and one person was in a bow tie, another in sweatpants, and a third in a leather jacket and cargo pants? This vision reminds me of the fashion in Arden's kindergarten class (although one might argue that showing up in an Elsa dress is taking things a step too far). The fashion sense of a five-year-old is so simple: "This outfit makes me happy!" No more, no less.

I invite you to dress for your inner five-year-old. And if anyone tries to tell you, "You'll do better work if you're dressed the part," just tell them:

"Actually, I get my best ideas in the shower..."

Try *Napoleon Dynamite*

You might think some professions are more amenable to fun at work than others. As in, maybe a creative agency can be cool and casual, but not us professional businesspeople doing professional business things. Our work is serious—much more akin to that of a surgeon.

When I think of a surgeon, I imagine someone with a furrowed brow demanding, "Scalpel!" with all seriousness of purpose. But do you know what world-renowned surgeons *actually* do in the OR?

They listen to *Napoleon Dynamite*.

Dr. Peter Attia, author of *Outlive* and former Johns Hopkins surgeon, recounts:

Surgeons are often listening to music in the OR, but we only listened to that CD [of Napoleon Dynamite clips]. For an entire month ... we never stopped laughing at this thing. People always ask when I tell this story, did it compromise the outcomes? And I will say that there was a period of three days when we did 13 kidney transplants: every one of those patients had a remarkable achievement outcome.

And not only was there *Napoleon Dynamite*, but there wasn't a zipper in sight! Why? Because the medical community knows the highest-stakes situations are no place for formality. Scrubs are sanitary and comfortable, and surgeons' brains work perfectly well when they are wearing them.

If surgeons can laugh in stretchy pants in an OR, you can definitely do the same in a budget meeting.

Deprofessionalize your team

If our teams are doing good, meaningful, challenging work in the world, isn't that enough? Let's not make the experience of work artificially uncomfortable if it doesn't need to be. Let it be easy. Let it be human.

Work doesn't need to look like "work" to be effective.

In fact, the times when your people are trying hard to make their work look like "work" are probably the times they lack confidence and don't feel the psychological safety to say so. Performative work is stressful and obscures conversations about what really matters. It's lipstick on a bar chart, so let's not expect it or praise it. Let's instead make quality work the goal and forget the rest.

One way to do this is to start inviting and modeling work that looks more human. On the next page is a completed worksheet you can use with your team or on your own. Scan the QR code for a blank copy.

Your brain works whether you're wearing a suit or stretchy pants

The business world says quality work looks like	When it can actually look like	I will encourage my people to embrace this by
Wearing blazers, pressed pants, sharp shoes, or a dark jean on a good day	Wearing pajamas or sequins, or working on your couch naked (camera off, please)	Wearing exercise clothes at the office if it makes it easier to exercise Complimenting someone's Hawaiian shirt Declaring a zipper-free day at the office
Using words like "bandwidth" and "core competencies"	Using words like "time" and "things we're good at"	Reviewing any email I send and deleting jargon Appointing a "talk like a human" editor Thinking about what I am going to say so I can speak simply and directly
Sitting at a desk outside of a 30-minute lunch break (if you're lucky)	Working in a park at a hotspot, getting a pedicure with a colleague during a one-on-one meeting, or taking a nap and coming back to a problem refreshed	Blocking time in my public calendar for a nap Asking for a phone call instead of a Zoom so I can walk while talking Inviting a colleague or team to work from a café or museum for the afternoon

If you need help generating ideas in column 1...

- Try doing a Google image search for "professional" and "business." What seems unnecessary, performative, or just silly?
- Imagine you wanted to impress someone in a job interview. What would you be inclined to wear, do, or say?

If you need help generating ideas in column 2...

- What's one way you like to work that could be considered non-standard?
- What have you always wanted to try at work, but you've been afraid of looking unprofessional?

If you need help generating ideas in column 3...

- What do you do at home when you're comfortable that you don't currently do at work?
- What would a five-year-old suggest you do?

Finally, review the ideas in column 3 and put an asterisk next to one to three ideas you want to try.

Closing thought

You may be reading all this and wondering if I'm trying to get you fired. Or at least an uncomfortable talking-to at work. Maybe you work in finance, and if you're not in slacks and a button-down, you might as well be wearing a clown suit. If it doesn't feel safe to show up to work without a zipper, then I challenge you to get creative—for your benefit and to model dissent for others. Maybe you find yourself some loafers that have a fuzzy lining. Maybe your button-down has a flamingo print. Or maybe you appreciate the straightforwardness of having a work uniform, in which case I urge you to be bold and add an emoji to your work email.

Show yourself and others that we can be humans at work.

Because we are.

3

SHOVELING SHIT IS FUN IF YOU LIKE YOUR CO-SHOVELERS

During the height of the pandemic, Brad and I binge watched *The Office* start to finish. It wasn't a conscious choice to pick a show about office work while we were quarantined, but I don't doubt our brains knew the show would be therapeutic.

In the show, the imaginary organization Dunder Mifflin is a paper sales company—an absolutely brilliant choice. If you were on *Family Feud* and the category was "dullest possible businesses," a fantastic guess would be paper sales. The point of the show was not to showcase purpose at work, or passion, or even the opposite, that work sucks. It was to show that, even without purpose and passion, work *doesn't* suck. And that's because of the people.

The office workers at Dunder Mifflin all kind of hated each other, except for a few notable romances, but they made their own fun, nonetheless. From the dullest of scenes—HR presentations, building fire safety protocols, and sales calls—came all kinds of hilarity. I'm very aware that some of the jokes didn't age well. But I think the sentiment remains: *Work is fun if we, together, make it that way.*

IN THIS CHAPTER

WORK IS SOMETHING WE DO WHILE WE'RE HANGING OUT ON THE PLANET[1]

You should like the people you spend your days with

Let me tell you about a few of the people I've been hanging out with (while, you know, making some work and money):

Sue has this uncanny way of slicing through all the bullshit of any project and getting to the heart of what our clients need. And when we start to spin and lose our way, she'll say, "The work will tell us what to do." She also has the most creative confidence of anyone I've ever known. If she sees an idea she thinks is good, get ready to do that idea! Her only major fault is that for some ungodly reason she spells "yay" as "yey." I adore her nonetheless.

Dini doesn't just care—he loves. When he writes, he *loves* those words and crafts them until they're right. He *loves* his teammates. And though everyone loves their family (mostly?), somehow he loves his with this rare ferocity. He loves paper planes, too. And building forts in the woods. And photography. Because now he's a photographer!

Huma is right about pretty much everything. She holds it all in her head. She knows what to do. She knows what other people need to know to do what they need to do. She can tell you what will happen two weeks from now and what you should be doing right now. When I work with Huma, I know everything will be okay. And when I follow her advice in life, I know it will be, too.

Matt makes me belly laugh every single day I work with him. He's endlessly cool in this retired lumberjack sort of way, which would make sense if you ever met him. He loves birding and well-crafted leather satchels and photography and physical newspapers. Most days I just want to be more like him, and so do our clients.

Jacques makes me feel understood. I think our brains run on the same frequency, because I can share some complex half-baked idea and he gets it. He will bravely say what he thinks even when it's hard. With his encouragement he makes *me* feel brave enough to say what I think (handy if you're writing a book). And if you're ever ordering food with Jacques, just get what he's getting.

Marc is my favorite scheming partner. No idea is too big for Marc, and not even in the "We can do it!" empty enthusiasm kind of way, but in the "I'll just ring up the CEO of [insert Fortune 100 company] and see if they want to partner" kind of way. He has the soul of an artist and the charm of a salesman, which means you're definitely going to be watching his screen-play one day.

Chris knows how to captivate. He's a visual magician. I can't count the number of times I've said to him, "I'm thinking this," and the next day he comes back with, "I'm thinking THIS," and it's 47x cooler. He also knows how to make pour-over coffee, and I know this because if you have a call with Chris before 10 am, he will almost certainly just be waking up.

If you've met me down here after skipping half the list, hello! I had those little colleague love letters in my head begging to get out, so thanks for allowing the space. (I had about 18 more for Caroline and Nancy and Jason and Erik and all the rest, but my wise editor Sarah said you probably got the idea after the third...) My point is that I love the people I work with. And the plainest I can say it is this:

I just want to hang around them.

There's a lot of debate about whether your coworkers can really be your friends. I suppose it depends on your definition of friend. I don't expect my colleagues to know me like my closest life-long friends, but I also don't think that means they're not my friends. I like them. I care about them. I know at least some things about their lives. I'd help them if they needed me. I want to spend time with them. And I do spend time with them— quite a lot sometimes. That's friendship enough for me!

So although you can follow all kinds of advice about how to pick a career or job (e.g., pick the work you love, pick the job you're most skilled at, pick a job with growth opportunities, pick the highest-paying job), my advice is this: figure out who you like hanging around, and then go work with them.

Because *you should like the people you spend your days with.*

Plain and simple!

Work can feel like hanging out

Sue: Milton believed that you spend so much time with the people you work with that you need to like them. Why would you want to spend time with people you didn't like? It's not complex. He had very long-term clients, like, relationships that were 25 years long. If he didn't really, truly like talking to the people he was around, that was a problem for him.

It was simple. Honestly, most of the time working with him felt like hanging out, and the work just sort of happened. The work was a by-product of hanging out.

Me: What do you miss most about Milton?

Sue: Milton was a genius on so many levels. I could share so many things that I miss about him. He was always very optimistic, incredibly imaginative, and a real mentor. We had a great friendship as well. What I miss most about that time at the studio, honestly, is just talking to him. Even over making work together. We would talk about everything, and he always had a perspective that was so wonderful to hear and so unique. Once I came to the studio and was feeling a bit paralyzed because my wife was taking an abrupt career detour to become a captain in the maritime industry from an established position in the wine industry. I am not very improvisational; I like the routine and predictability of life. When I was telling Milton about my wife's sudden change, he said, "Sue, what she really wants is the feeling of the wind in her hair, smelling the water, seeing the open skies. It's not rational, but it is real." Only he would have responded like that. I miss that so much, on a very deep level. That's what I love most about him. The conversation about the complexity of people, the understanding of the world, the nuances of society.

....

Even when you work with a genius doing society-shifting work, one thing holds true: *the relationships mean the most.*

Fun beats mandates every time

By now perhaps it's crossed your mind: Bree, where are all these good laughs happening? On Zoom in 30-minute meetings after you've covered the main agenda?

Since we're now three chapters into a book about work, maybe it's time to wind our way to the never-ending debate about *where* work happens. For those who need to move physical things as part of their role, then of course they need to be where those things are. In this section (and largely in this book) I'm speaking about knowledge workers who move ideas. Let's enter via a story.

As I've mentioned before, my first full-time job was teaching middle school math. It was super tempting to try and mandate student engagement with admonishments like "Stop doodling or I'll ask you to leave!" "Sit still, look forward!" But if you've ever been a teacher (or had a teacher like that), you'll know that this strategy is a race to the bottom. It becomes a power struggle and promotes sneaky behavior. And one thing it *definitely* doesn't help with is student engagement. It helps only with the *appearance* of engagement. You can indeed control whether someone sits still and looks at you. You cannot, however, control whether they're listening or instead itemizing the fashion mistakes they think you made this morning.

So what do you do instead? How do you get all those hormone-fueled, distracted 13-year-olds to get excited about triangles? My mentor that year, the teaching sage Lyle Hatridge, taught me this:

"The best classroom management is a great lesson plan."

In other words, if you plan a captivating class full of a motley assortment of inspiration, surprise, reflection, social learning, competition, and creativity, you have no need for mandates. It's just *fun*. It's the teachers that lecture for 50 minutes and expect rigorous note-taking that have trouble.

What does this have to do with the debate over who works where and who decides? If the work you have people doing is inherently fun and the team genuinely enjoys spending time with each other, you don't have to mandate shit.

Because mandates stink. Do you like when people mandate something of you? What does it do to your sense of autonomy, pride, and engagement? How about your sense of resentment toward the mandate-er? To hark back to my student engagement story, in which class do you remember being most engaged? The one with the strictest teacher? Or the one who operated with the assumption that learning was fascinating and you'd love it, too?

BetterUp surveyed 1,400 full-time US employees who were mandated to return to the office and found they had higher levels of burnout, stress, and turnover intentions. They also had lower levels of trust in their organization, engagement, and productivity. Gallup found that commutes of only 30 minutes are linked to higher levels of stress and anger, and commutes of 45 minutes or more are linked to poorer overall well-being, daily mood, and health.

Those are some high prices to pay! What do we do instead?

First, we should remember that physical distance does not imply emotional distance. Perhaps the closest project team I ever led was when we were 100 percent remote early in the pandemic.

But second, I get that a company feels so much more alive when people are together, at least some of the time. I love going into the office! If that's what you want, then this is what you should do:

Drop the mandates: Not five days or three days or two days or one. Just say, "Work in the space that is best for your brain! Maybe that's the office, your bed, a park, or while you're hanging out at a colleague's apartment. Maybe it's while you're getting a pedicure!" (Highly recommended; my friend Lisa's brilliant idea.)

The quality
of your
relationships
    determines
    the quality
of your life.

ESTHER PEREL

Hang out in person occasionally: Maybe your team comes together once a year, or maybe it's the kickoff of every new quarter or project. The more frequently you want to come together, though, the better it's done at the local team level so everyone can decide together what works. I've led several teams that were New York–based and decided to work in the office together most days just because we liked it. No guilt. No mandate. We just did what we thought would make it a good day.

Create the great lesson plan: Now, for the love of all things good, if you are meeting in person, let the time be fun! This doesn't mean a structured-down-to-the-minute offsite. It could be a loosely structured day of jamming together, or a series of one-on-one walks to punctuate a day of co-working while you enjoy the free snacks. It could be a day of doing things that take full advantage of being with your people in the third dimension: drawing on whiteboards, sketching prototypes, playing a soundtrack in the background, shooting paper airplanes at each other. Do not under any circumstance ask people to come into an office and then spend the entire time on calls.

Be cool: I don't know any other way to say this, but, are you a good hang? I don't mean this at all in the way people tell women to smile or that you have to be some kind of cruise director—none of that. There is no one right way to be cool. I just mean that *you* probably want to hang around people who are fun to hang out with, and so a really good way to get people together is to be one of those people yourself. Do you laugh at people's jokes? Laugh at yourself? Make people feel seen and appreciated? Show up in your stretchy pants—literal or figurative—so your team members don't feel the need to put on their business masks either? No one wants to commute with the reward being even more code switching.

When Sue and I were planning our first Do Nothing Day (see chapter 4), I said my goal for the day was for it to be everyone's *best day at work ever*. Make no small plans, right? And you know what we heard after? Many people said, "That was one of my best days at work ever." Sure they snuck in the words "one of," but I'll take it!

It is so very different from tracking badge swipes.

Friendship is good for ~~business~~ life

Hi, everyone. This is the practical side of Bree's brain taking over the keyboard because the rest of Bree has refused to make the business case for anything. That's laudable, for sure, but it would also be nice if a CPO or CEO wanted to buy this book. Understandably, they are responsible for the business, so I've commandeered this section to give the business case for liking the people you work with.

Gallup has produced some impressive research in this area, repeatedly showing that "having a best friend at work is strongly linked to business outcomes, including profitability, safety, inventory control, and retention."

I know, "inventory control"? Go figure.

Further, "Employees who have a best friend at work are significantly more likely to

- engage customers and internal partners;
- get more done in less time . . .;
- innovate and share ideas."

So there you have it, friendship is good for business.

Pay no attention to the muffled yell from real Bree, coming from the trunk of my imaginary car... "FRIENDSHIP IS GOOD FOR ENJOYING YOUR LIFE!"

Luckily, both can be true.

The best teams are cozy teams

At this very moment I'm sitting in sweatpants on my couch watching the fog roll through the city, cat snuggled up on my right. It's a safe, calming, "this is enough" kind of feeling.

This morning I woke up and looked out to a 7 am that looked more like a grumpy 5 am and wondered how I could arrange to stay in bed all day. But alas there was a child and an animal who both insisted on eating. Brad and I did the breakfasting and the walking to school, I did the emails and the Slacks, but I did not manage to do the showering before the Zoom team meeting.

We started with a check-in (later in this chapter I'll explain how), as we always do, and I was able to say, "I'm a four. I haven't showered, but also I don't care. Thank you for making it okay for me to not care and for accepting me as I am!"

Luckily, my brain works no matter if my hair is freshly washed or a total mess.

(For the record, I do shower if I'm going to see people in 3D. That's just a good life rule.)

I was able to show up as I did because I love our team. It's a cozy team. We do amazing work, and we get to be humans while we do it. Some other benefits of cozy teams:

Cozy teams help each other in times of need. One person is drowning in work? The team comes to the rescue to pull more weight or redistribute. One person is sick or going through something hard? The team does whatever it can to ease the burden.

Cozy teams say thanks and sorry. Thanks for helping me. Thanks for pushing the work. Thanks for telling me how you were feeling. Thanks for listening. Sorry for making that confusing. Sorry for being a little grumpy. Sorry for not communicating earlier.

Cozy teams share crazy ideas. They're not bound by some notion of what normal work looks like. They're free to share ridiculous, unreasonable ideas, and they try to figure out together how they can make the ridiculous, unreasonable ideas a reality.

Cozy teams have good days. They like hanging around each other, in some part, because collaborating in person is productive. But they also like hanging around each other because they like hanging around each other.

Cozy teams do amazing work. It's not that there aren't crises to manage or pivots to make or work to push to the next level. It's that cozy teams know how to navigate those things together and want each other by their side through the journey.

I'll write more in the next section about how to create a cozy team, but right now that same child that wanted breakfast also wants to be picked up from school—can you even imagine. I'll be back.

HOW TO LEAD A COZY TEAM

Treat people as high performers who care

There is no cozy team without trust.

You know the opposite of coziness? Power struggles. Side-eye and resentment are categorically un-cozy.

Here is an eye-opener: just 12 percent of leaders say they have full confidence their team is productive in a hybrid environment.

I'm sorry, but something is very wrong here. Twelve percent?! No wonder leaders are grasping to get people in offices; they want to physically confirm their productivity. This is a race to the bottom if I ever saw one.

Yes, the basic economics of work assume the employer tries to get the most work out of an employee while paying as little as they can get away with. Similarly, employers often assume their employees try to do the least amount of work while being paid the most they can get in the market. Fundamentally, it's a trade.

Time is money, money is time, right?

But what if that's a bad system? A system based on distrust and the maximal extraction of the other party. What if instead we had a system, or at least a subculture at the team level, that was based on trust and generosity?

Let's assume that not always, but occasionally, evening work is necessary for your business. Even if you try your best to create a culture of sustainability and pace the work appropriately, inevitably at some point something needs to be redone, there's a dependency you didn't realize, or something just takes longer than you thought. It happens.

In those moments, as a leader, you hope your team will show up for you and for the work. That showing up has a cost, but you determine that pulling someone away from their dinner or child or sleep is, on this occasion, worth it. You're taking a withdrawal from that person. The only way that's even slightly okay is if you've already made the deposits.

In the same way that great work sometimes requires investment from people to go "above and beyond," it's also true that sometimes the work slows. It could be a break between projects, waiting for another team to deliver something you need, or simply a canceled meeting.

In those scenarios, a leader's job is to FIGHT THE INSTINCT to pull more work from the backlog. Anyone can invent more work or find something that would be "good to do." But that's the exact opposite of what you should do in these moments. Instead, we should all see these moments as opportunities to make a deposit.

What does that look like? Saying,

- "We're good for today . . . go sign off!"
- "We don't need anything at the moment. Go take a nap!"
- "I've got it from here. Go fish! Or whatever else you feel like."

As a leader, I'm always trying to maximize the quality of work *and* minimize the amount of work the team is doing. If spending time on something is not going to meaningfully increase the quality of work, then my goal is to return that time to the individual. Don't get me wrong, often it feels impossible to do for long stretches, but it's still my goal. And when I do feel the need to ask for something at 9 pm, I hope that that person knows I'm not trying to extract more from them—I'm asking out of a meaningful need. And I try my best to make those occasions rare.

I'm using the language "deposit and withdrawal" because I find it catchy. But make no mistake, I don't believe this to be clever transactional advice for leaders to get their people to work evenings. It's not a trick. It's a genuine belief that the amount of work someone does should balance out to the hours you agreed to. If you know you will occasionally have to eat into your people's non-business hours, then you'd better give some business hours back. This advice is also born from my annoyance with the busywork that arises from "well, this person has some time, we might as well give them something to do that could possibly create value."

Instead of always trying to extract more, what happens when we try to do our best for each other? What if it's the team's job to take care of creating brilliant work and having the leader's back, and it's the leader's job to take care of the team and keep overwork to a minimum?

It works only if everyone is in it. The leader who starts prioritizing the work at a regular cost to the team's nights and weekends will soon find themselves with a team that learns they have to prioritize themselves or no one else will. And conversely, a team that doesn't truly care about the work, the leader, or ideally both will find itself with a leader who feels they have to demand time and care or they won't get it.

The trick is that no one wants to be the one who begins this cycle of generosity for fear that they'll be taken advantage of. The team member fears if they put in extra hours and overdeliver, they'll only be met with a leader who says, "Thank you," and now expects that regularly. The leader fears if they allow for downtime, they're not getting the full value of an employee, they're not doing their best by the business, and maybe employees will start to always expect to do less.

It reminds me of the successful game theory strategy "tit for tat."

Under tit for tat, a player will begin by cooperating, then in subsequent iterations will replicate whatever their opponent did last time. So if their initial cooperation is punished with defection, they will then reciprocate in kind.

Put simply, it means that in a cooperative system, the best strategy is to start with generosity. Only if someone takes advantage do you switch to looking out for yourself. If we assume some employees really are trying to do the minimum, well, "fool me once...," as they say. But even with that risk, game theory teaches us that it's *still* the best strategy to start with generosity. Or in other words, treat all your employees as high performers who care, advocate for their naps, and deal with any underperformers on a case-by-case basis.

If game theory isn't your thing but classic Christmas movies are, it reminds me of the scene at the end of *It's a Wonderful Life* when George Bailey finds himself broke and the entire town shows up for him with cash and money wires and gold watches. That happened because he had spent his life making literal deposits in his community in the form of home loans and emotional deposits in the form of kindness. Did Mr. Potter successfully extract more material riches from his people and customers? Certainly. But, in the end, it's George Bailey who ends up "the richest man in town."

That's the kind of leader I hope to be.

Breaks my heart
that pirates spend
their whole lives following
a map, when the real
treasure is the
friendships they
build along the way.

Have each others' backs

"Bree, what if you need the team to work more, push harder, and they're just not?"

Well, then, you tell the truth. This is what I've said in this kind of scenario:

"Team, I'm scared. We promised to deliver x by y for the client, and I'm worried we're not going to make it. And worried that even if we do, it won't be our best work. I was the one who scoped this work, so I'm really sorry if I scoped badly and didn't give us enough time and didn't anticipate the detours we've had. I own that. But nevertheless, here we are. I know you've all been working hard and are good at what you do. Which is why I don't want to ask for us to push even harder and eat into our evenings. I will do whatever I can to pull as much weight as I can. I'm really happy to take xyz on myself to lighten the load. I want us all to be proud of what we produce, and I also don't want to burn us out. I'm really open to any ideas anyone has about the best way to get us to 'done and successful' while still taking care of ourselves."

I don't think I've had a single team who hasn't told me in response:

"We've got you, Bree. We're in it together. Whoever can stay late tonight will stay and do a big push. Who wants to order dinner?"

No mandate. No side-eye. No guilt. Just genuine teamwork and care. Many of my teams have told me, "This is the most psychologically safe team of my career." That may sound boastful, but I tell you this because I want every leader to trust their teams, and I want every team to trust their leader. I want that 12 percent to be 100 percent. I want teams to tell me, "Our team has so much trust," and have that be totally average.

Shoot straight, with love

Maybe you're thinking, "Bree, I hear you. Tell the truth. Try some of
the vulnerability Brené is always on about. But what if one of my team
members really does suck? Like, they're not pulling their weight or maybe
they're just not good at their job, or maybe they're causing problems in
the team. What, I just love them into greatness?"

Of course not. If there's really a problem and it's making it hard to create
or maintain a cozy and effective team, do this first: talk to the person
one-on-one as soon as possible.

That same year I was teaching seventh grade math, I had a student I'll
call Anthony. He was a total flirt with the girls, constantly disruptive in
class, and generally my nemesis. I tried asking him to leave the class.
I tried ignoring him. I even tried playing along. Nothing was working.
That's when Lyle, my mentor, said to me, "Have you tried talking to him?"

Well, sure, it sounds obvious when you say it like that . . .

I remember it like it was yesterday. After class I discreetly asked Anthony
if he would walk with me around the building to a quiet spot. I opened
the conversation by letting him know I liked him and that I knew he was a
good kid. And then I asked, "What's going on?"

He immediately apologized. He knew. When he was separated from all
those seventh-grade ladies he was trying to impress, he didn't feel the
need to show up so *big*. He went from being a class clown to a kid. I told
him how his outbursts were affecting the class. He said he'd stop. I told
him again that I liked him and believed in him. From then on we had a
connection, and he knew I saw him. He reined in his antics for the rest of
the year. And the truth is, I really *did* like him! He was a funny kid with a
real fire in him, who is . . . oh god . . . a 30-something man now. Anthony,
if you're reading this, I hope you're doing well!

The point is that the best strategy is to always believe your people are good. Good and misunderstood maybe. Good and in the wrong role. Good and overwhelmed. Good and feeling insecure. Good and lost. Good and without the right skills. It just takes an honest, loving conversation to figure out which it is.

Once you know, you can do one of two things:

1. Repair the rift
For example, maybe they didn't fully understand the team priorities and need support understanding what's important and urgent. Or maybe they're overwhelmed with caregiving responsibilities and need some flexibility this month. Or maybe they have a specific skill gap that you're willing to help them fill. If that doesn't work . . .

2. Fire them, with love
Sometimes you might help them find a better fit in a role elsewhere in the organization. Other times, it's just not going to work, and that's okay. I'm not a fan of long, drawn-out "performance improvement plans" that hold someone static in a role on some kind of amorphous probation. It feels icky for everyone. Sure, in some cases it's worth giving someone a chance with direct feedback and quick support. But if you know in your bones it's just not going to work, then gather the most generous severance you can and cut the person loose to find a role that's better for them. You owe it to that person, and to the rest of the team who has likely been picking up that person's slack.

It's no fun, to be sure. But drowning yourself and the team because it's too hard isn't any better.

Try three team rituals

I've covered distrust, fear, and slackers in this super fun section about cozy teams. Shall we turn our attention to getting cozy and basking in the warm glow of collaboration? Let's do it.

I have three things for you to do that will get you 80 percent of the way to having the coziest team around.

According to *Forbes*, leadership development is a $366 billion global industry. Sure, a lot of leaders need support on everything from setting a vision to managing P&Ls, but when it comes to creating safe, joyful, high-performing teams, if everyone just did these three things, I'm pretty sure we could save, like, $300 billion. Plus, they're fun! Let's give them their own sections:

- The user manual (annually or to kick off a new team)
- The check-in (daily)
- The fast food rule (in every one-on-one situation)

Swap user manuals

It's much easier to like the people you work with if you actually know them. It's amazing to me how you can work with someone for years and not know even basic things about them like if they have siblings. Some argue that information about family and friends and life outside of work is too personal to share or ask about. I'm not advocating for sharing stories about losing your virginity here, just having the very most basic understanding of who the human is across from you. Like, what city do they live in? Do they have a pet? Knowing someone at this basic level is, well, just nice.

There's also knowing what someone needs and how they show up as a team member. In most teams, you kind of figure out over the course of years and trial and error whether someone needs alone time if they're stressed or if they need to talk it out. But why can't we short circuit that? Can't we just ask?

As a quick aside, this relevant post made me guffaw: "BREAKING: My husband was just talking to a casual acquaintance whose name he couldn't remember, so he said, 'I'm sorry, I forget your name?' and the guy told him his name. I didn't know you could do that??"

Turns out that we can! And we should.

Imagine buying a fancy new blender with all sorts of buttons and symbols. You could just *guess* how to use it, but why? It comes with a user manual and probably even a quick start guide. Why can't people come with the same?

Enter the user manual: a guide for how to "operate" you, written by you for your teammates.

I've been using user manuals with teams for over a decade (I first picked up the practice in grad school), and sharing them goes well 100 percent of the time.

Here's what you need to know about working with user manuals.

When to create a user manual

- If you're popping up a new team like we do in consulting, write and share user manuals live at the start of a new project.
- For ongoing teams, create team user manuals once, then revisit them yearly, with any new team members sharing theirs when they join.

How to create a user manual

- Set up your team user manuals in a shared Google Doc or another editable, sharable system with one template per person.

- Ask everyone on the team to fill out theirs independently.

- Schedule a 60- to 90-minute user manual session in which you share your responses live with each other. This is *important*. User manuals fall in the category of important but not urgent, so if you merely ask people to read others' manuals on their own, they will never prioritize it.

- In the session, encourage each person to share their answers one at a time. If you have a huge team, you can ask people to share any three or four responses they choose. I've also done this with teams in a "speed dating" style, where pairs ask questions from the user manuals that they want to know about each other, and after five minutes, they switch pairs.

What to include in your user manual

The table on the facing page is a sample user manual with my answers included so you can see how it goes. Follow the QR code for a template you can copy, as well as alternate questions.

P.S. This is not a bad exercise to use on a date, but I'll leave it to you to adapt the questions and give it a go if you have the opportunity.

My fullest name	Bree Andrea Groff
The people and/or animals most central in my life are	My husband, Brad; my daughter, Arden; my dad, Mark (he has Alzheimer's, and I take care of things for him since I am an only child); my two closest friends, Lizzie and Jenessa. My mom passed away in 2022, and I think about her every day. Also in my life are our cats Ava and Tessie and the dogs Charlie and Sadie that used to be my parents' and are now my in-laws' dogs but whom we dog-sit a lot. I'm pretty sure I'm my vet's best customer, but it's really a joy.
The biggest commitments and/or joys outside of work right now are	I'm writing a book (as in, like, right now), I take care of and enjoy time with my dad, I spend time with Arden, and I'm super into health and longevity these days, so lots of exercise. Also Agatha Christie mysteries.
It makes me happy in a team when	We're enjoying each other and the process, while doing work we're really proud of. When we're not taking ourselves too seriously.
What I don't have patience for on a team is	When there's unspoken resentment brewing or when people aren't considering the needs of others on the team.
How you can help when I'm stressed or stuck	I usually need to talk my way through my feelings and ideas, so if you can say something like, "Hey, what's going on? Can I listen?" I'd be so grateful.
I'm pretty good at _____ so you can lean on me to _____	I'm good at facilitation and client relationships, so you can lean on me to lead a meeting in a pinch and work through any hiccups with the client on our behalf.
At work, I'm trying to get really good at	Creating more space for others to lead client moments. Sometimes I can over-flex the muscle I just described above.
What excites me about this [project/team/quarter/client/ initiative] is	This dream team! I was so excited to get this group of superstars together, some of whom I've worked with before, and some I don't know whose stellar reputations precede you.
What makes work joyful and sustainable for me is	I may or may not have written a book about this . . .
Bonus: My birthday is (optional)	March 20th (and I like it when people say happy birthday!)

Do a daily check-in

Having an aligned and joyful team is pretty simple. But somehow the norms of business productivity have squeezed out all the human juice that makes a team work well. Take, for example, just starting a team meeting with "How are you?" instead of "Okay, let's jump right in." You may think the jumping-in method is more efficient, but I can tell you confidently it is *not* more effective. You know what *is* effective? An aligned and joyful team. And that comes from acknowledging each other as humans first, before using each other as work-bots. At its heart, the check-in is just a structured way of asking each person on the team, "How are you?" and actually inviting them to share. In return, you are actually listening. Here's how it works.

At your daily stand-up or at the top of your regular meetings (no more than once a day), ask:

"How is everyone? On the count of three, we'll all hold a hand up with the number of fingers that represents how we are (from zero to five). It can be how you're feeling about work, about life, about anything, just—how are you? Okay, one, two, three, shoot!"

You may get some twos, a five, and a few in between. Then, ask everyone to share why they chose that number in thirtyish seconds each. Perhaps they're at a two because they're stressed about a meeting later, or they're at a five because it's their birthday this weekend, or they're a three because they just realized they're wearing two different socks.

Tactically, the PM or I usually count us down, then we see all the fingers, then the PM or I will nominate one person to start. After they share, they nominate the next person, and on it goes until everyone has shared. The check-in is best done in team/meeting sizes of four to ten people and takes maybe five to ten minutes. If you start it right when the meeting begins, even if people are still joining, you're likely to start the "work" part of the meeting no later than if you had just casually chatted waiting for others to join.

The practice has about a bajillion benefits, but I'll outline some here:

1 **Psychological safety:** When you practice sharing your thoughts and feelings and are met with support from teammates, you're more likely to do it again, even when it's harder.

2 **Cognitive offloading:** Like shutting down non-essential apps so your computer runs faster, verbalizing what's running in the back of your mind (e.g., I'm nervous about that meeting, I'm excited about my birthday, WTF is up with these socks) helps you to then focus on the work at hand.

3 **Thwarting misunderstanding:** If someone shows up to a virtual meeting camera-off, you might wonder if they're paying attention and committed, but if they were to say, "Team, I'm a two today. My back is killing me, so I'm joining this meeting horizontally," you've now dodged the side-eye and replaced it with empathy.

4 **Inclusive teams:** How often have you been in a meeting where one or more people literally said nothing the entire time? Have you ever been that person and thought, "Oh god, I want to say this thing, but if it's the only thing I say this whole meeting, it better be good..." Ensuring that every person has spoken up within the first 10 minutes of the meeting can reduce the barrier to them speaking up again.

5 **It's just fucking nice:** It's nice to care about how each other is doing, it's nice to be cared about, and 30 seconds of listening to someone is not going to be a drain on your team or business, I promise you.

Finally, I've found the check-in to be the most effective (and efficient!) way to reproduce some of the *The Office* camaraderie vibes in virtual and hybrid teams. In one team, we got to hear the daily play-by-play of our colleague, Joher, buying a house. It was a fantastic tale of will-they-won't-they as he navigated contracts and fishy sellers and performed high-wire acts of rerouting money. We heard all about his eventual move-in and his adventures in weed-whacking, which we learned is legally mandatory in California. Every day his check-in was like a real estate telenovela. It was entertaining to be sure, but also made us all feel closer, as witnesses to each other's lives.

Good laughs with good people.

We did kickass work, too!

P.S. I'm a five! I get to write most of the day today, which feels like a great luxury. I just ate a delicious avocado toast with sprouts. And my coffee shop barista friend Xandi just said hi, which makes my day. What's your number?

Use the fast food rule

This concept comes from child development specialist Dr. Harvey Karp. (It's pretty amazing how much parenting philosophy and management philosophy go hand in hand, as potentially offensive as that may be.)

When you're meeting with someone one-on-one and your team member is telling you about something that upset them, you might feel the instinct to help them see why they shouldn't feel so upset. Unfortunately, according to Dr. Karp, and likely your own experience, "Agitated people are terrible listeners."

Or maybe they're telling you about a win, and you're super excited to jump in with a story about a similar win you had! All very normal. And also, likely, not at all what your team member needs.

Consider a fast food drive-through: You pull up and say, "I'll have a burger, a shake, and a side of fries, please." What's the first thing the server says back? It's not "Would you like to supersize that?" or "Please pull ahead." And it's definitely not "You're wrong, that's not a good order." It's this: "Okay, I've got one burger, a shake, and a side of fries."

Before anything else, they make sure YOU are heard. It's lovely!

If your team member is telling you that they're feeling lost about the direction of the work and they are unsure about the upcoming meeting, before jumping into why they should feel great about it, try saying, "I think I see. You're worried about the direction of our work, and particularly about how that shows up at our next meeting. Did I get it right?"

In my experience, people will then usually expand: "Yes, that's right. I've been feeling like this for some time, and..."

The fast food rule is one of the best antidotes to having a shitty team. Because the worst kind of team isn't one where the work is tedious or the client is difficult or business is down. The worst kind of team is one where it doesn't feel like a team at all: where you feel alone, misunderstood, underappreciated, and unsupported. Taking that off the table gets you 95 percent of the way there, every time.

Closing thought

I'm a big fan of work happy hours, dinners, holiday parties, and the like. I'm even pro-ping pong tables, even though they've become the poster child for faking a good culture (because, hello, ping pong is fun). But all those things are just icing on the work friendship cake.

Real friendship—*good laughs with good people*—comes from moving through work and life together.

That's why this chapter isn't filled with party-planning ideas, but methods for genuinely getting to know each other, for bearing witness to each other's lives day in and day out, and for building a shared understanding of what you're all going through.

There's a reason war buddies aren't called war colleagues. When you're really in it with each other, friendship grows.

4

MAKE BRILLIANT WORK—DON'T LET BUSYNESS AND CONFORMITY SABOTAGE YOU

I'm sitting in the aptly named "sitting room" in a beautiful upstate NY retreat. I've taken myself on a little writer's getaway because, although I love my usual coffee shop with the great breakfast quesadillas, sometimes you need a change of scenery to do great work. Brad, thank you for holding down our Manhattan fort with Arden while I'm here, hopefully making brilliant work for a chapter titled, "Make brilliant work." No pressure.

I woke up this morning like a kid on Christmas, so excited to pack for this trip. I exercised six out of seven days during this past week because I wanted to be in peak physical and mental condition and awash in inspiration. I packed my pouches of vegetable smoothies and other assorted supplements that I've become super nerdy about recently.

I also gathered up all the books, notebooks, and writer's accoutrements that I thought might provide me with inspiration. On the drive, I alternated between belting out Beyoncé's "Check on It" and "Pennies from Heaven" by Louis Prima, Sam Butera, and The Witnesses. Brad can attest that I'm very happy listening to one or two songs over and over again for hours. See? I'm a great hang.

Let's now fast forward to the point after I arrived, when instead of writing for the first two hours, I ordered chocolate milk in bulk for Arden, watched a video of Taylor Swift talking about how she wrote the song "Lover," and researched the health benefits of chia seeds. Not the start I was after.

I tell you all of this because inspired work is elusive and requires the right conditions. It's hard to conjure. Hard to wrangle into the 30-minute block you have before your next meeting. And it definitely doesn't happen when you're sleep deprived and hungry. My muse is not impressed with corporate working norms, and I'm guessing yours isn't either.

In fact, Taylor Swift told me in that video that I watched, "I've never really been able to fully explain songwriting other than it's like this little glittery cloud floats in front of your face and you grab it at the right time and then you revert back to what you know about the structure of a song in order to fill in the gaps."

Look at that. Turns out that two hours wasn't a total waste!

Anyway, of course not all work requires divine inspiration. Some stuff is just stuff that needs to happen to keep the wheels moving. Some stuff is even important, but a tried-and-true strategy for dealing with it is plenty good enough. And to clarify, I don't believe all brilliant work comes from sitting in a sitting room waiting for inspiration. Sometimes it comes through conversation or trying things out.

You know, there's enough clarifying to do here that maybe I should make one of those "In/Out" lists that are popular with the kids on social media. Shall we try?

In	Out
Two-plus-hour blocks on your calendar just for thinking	Having to wait until everyone's asleep or no one is yet awake to do any real thinking
Do Nothing Days, offsites, retreats	30-minute "brainstorm" meetings
Saying what you think!	Trying to make your work look "normal"
Project plans that include time for inspiration and debate	Project plans that include time only for cranking
Treating your instrument (your brain!) like a Stradivarius violin	Shoving calories and/or caffeine into your instrument just to keep it functional
Moving your body to help you think	Sitting at a desk for eight hours a day, and the associated hunchbacks that come with that (not healthy nor sexy)
Entertaining yourself with your work	Putting yourself to sleep with your own work
Honing your craft	Getting to done

I choose "In"!

IN THIS CHAPTER

MAKING BRILLIANT WORK SHOULD FEEL GOOD

Brilliance does not require pain
....

Your body is an instrument
....

Don't break the instruments
....

Why do brilliant work?
....

Work can make us feel alive
....

Make work that wows
....

The barriers to brilliant work
....

Normal work is never brilliant
....

The value of an unspoiled mind
....

Brilliance loves absurdity:
The bakery
....

Genius can exist in
everyday business
....

Who is doing the brilliant
thinking and when?
....

We make ourselves
busy and normal
....

Meet the boss of work
....

HOW TO DO LESS, BETTER WORK

Amuse yourself
....

Revere your ideas
....

Know your muse
....

Sit and think
....

Have a Do Nothing Day
....

Design brilliance into
your day-to-day
....

MAKING BRILLIANT WORK SHOULD FEEL GOOD

Brilliance does not require pain

That might be a controversial thing to say because we are constantly fed the idea that "nothing worth doing is easy."

I don't know... have you ever tried making a baby?

Sure, the raising-a-child part is a bit of a lift, but at least for some, the making part is less so!

That idea that "nothing worth doing is easy" is just not strictly true. It isn't *always* easy to be sure, but it's definitely not *always* hard. We have to stop equating struggle with greatness. It's a recipe for performative exhaustion.

Greg McKeown, author of *Effortless*, articulates this perfectly:

What if the biggest thing keeping us from doing what matters is the false assumption that it has to take tremendous effort? What if, instead, we considered the possibility that the reason something feels hard is that we haven't yet found the easier way to do it?

And when there *is* struggle, the quality of that struggle matters. The pursuit of greatness, when it *is* hard, should feel like the good kind of pain.

When you're working in pursuit of something that truly lights you up— whether because of the challenge, how you can flex your skills, the potential for impact, the people you're doing it with, or something else— the pain should feel like a hard workout. It's something you chose. An opportunity to prove yourself. Something you know will be worth it. Something you've trained for. Something you know is ultimately good for you.

It should not feel like getting beat up. That's a bad kind of pain.

If the struggle does make you feel really awful, it's likely because you *didn't* choose to be working at 1 am, but your boss or team or client expected you to deliver. It's not an opportunity to prove yourself, just to do damage control so someone doesn't get upset. It might be truly stupid work that you know won't make a difference. It may be work that is beyond your skills and you're not prepared or equipped or supported to do what's asked. And nothing about this feels good for you.

The distinction is this:

Do you feel like you're *on fire?* Or do you feel burned to a crisp?

Your body is an instrument

If you're going to do brilliant work, you better know what you're workin' with.

Professional violinists invest in the world's finest instruments. Once they go through the thousands of hours of practicing intently for years on end, it makes absolutely no sense to have that skill diminished on a less-than-stellar instrument.

And yet, for you, a knowledge worker, do you know what your instrument is? *Your body.* I won't even say your mind, because so many of us are used to thinking of our minds as separate from our bodies. Nope, your instrument is in fact that fleshy, wrinkly lump inside your skull, which is 100 percent part of your body.

And yet . . . how much caffeine do we chug? How much sleep do we forgo? How much exercise do we skip? How often do we mindlessly down empty calories just to keep ourselves going at our desks? We might have spent hundreds of thousands of dollars on an education, but we're playing violin on a cardboard box with rubber bands.

And worse, we do it with pride!

I'll admit I've often felt the honor that comes with back-to-backs and late nights and exhaustion. But imagine instead that you're in the orchestra pit and you say to your fellow musicians, "My violin is so smashed today it's barely working. I just rubbed some motor oil on it to spruce up the wood—it's all I could grab in a pinch. Okay, when should we start warming up?"

It would be shocking! Do you not have any respect for the one thing that allows you to do your work?! You may think you can perform just the same, but you definitely can't.

According to *Harvard Business Review*, "Lack of sleep leads to detriments in job performance, productivity, career progression, and satisfaction, and an increase in job-related accidents, absenteeism, and counterproductive work behaviors."

Looking at charisma and inspiration, Chris Barnes of the University of Washington found that "sleep-deprived leaders tend to be less charismatic (meaning they will have a harder time inspiring their teams), and sleep-deprived team members attribute less charisma to their leaders (meaning that they are more difficult to inspire)."

In other words, you're worse at your job and no one's impressed.

Okay, I got a little ranty there, but the rant was more at the way we "do business," not at you. I know, you may have little control over all of those back-to-back meetings or when someone expects a thing of you. You can't just invent time! And you're doing your best. When work takes everything from you during the day, the last thing you want to do is have a salad and exercise. No. I will take the chips and queso, please.

My hope is that we can make this situation better, together. You and me. I'll write this book and try to get it out to as many people as possible. And you try to use your leadership and power and personal boundaries to take good care of your Stradivarius and those of your team. You in?

Don't break the instruments

I can't help but feel that offering robust employee benefits to a population of overworked employees is like ransacking someone's house and then giving them a voucher for a broom so they can clean it up.

Can we just, like, not destroy people's well-being in the first place?

What if companies offered a basic benefits package with great healthcare but nothing fancy beyond that, and then took the savings and did one of these three things, every year:

1 Reduce company revenue targets so people aren't having to push so hard.
2 Return that savings straight to employee paychecks.
3 Hire more people to ease the load of current employees.

Because you know what's better than a reduced gym membership fee? *Actually having time to go to the gym.*

I imagine a world where our employer doesn't need to be everything to us—our meal plan, the sum of our friendships, our health care, therapy, religion, and sense of identity. For the same reason you probably don't want to share a bank account with someone you may only date a couple of years, having your life intricately intertwined with an organization creates a dependency that's hard to break free from—both logistically and psychologically. In all aspects of life, our ability to set and keep boundaries is in direct proportion to the confidence we have in our own independence.

I think it's possible that the best thing an employer can do sometimes is to be *less* to its people.

Just be a *really great job.*

There are three
responses to a piece
of design—yes,
no, and wow!
Wow is the
one to aim for.

MILTON GLASER

Why do brilliant work?

It's worth asking why. I see three answers, and they're not mutually exclusive:

1 Do brilliant work to grow a high-performing, healthy business.
2 Do brilliant work to create impact in the world.
3 Do brilliant work because it's one of the coolest parts of being human.

I've made a living as a management consultant, so I've thought a lot about #1. It was in fact my job to make #1 true for my clients. You might say, "Come on, Bree. We all know this one is really 'Do brilliant work to make money in a capitalist society.'" Sure. But I see that as an externality of #1.

I believe healthy, high-performing businesses matter. Business at its simplest is just a structure we use so we can all work together and not have it be all *Lord of the Flies*. I've been a CEO and know what it means to financially sustain a business. I've advised many powerful business leaders, and I know the pressure on their shoulders with sometimes hundreds of thousands of jobs to support. Also, I have an unfortunate fondness for travel and fancy bar soap and overpriced socks, so I am a fan of making money. Yes, #1 is a good reason to make brilliant work.

But it's not my favorite…

Creating impact in the world is a good one, too. Some people would even argue it's the only reason. Some work, of course, is highly positively impactful to humanity. Even companies that make quality overpriced socks are bringing joy to someone. I have no beef with impact. It's critical! But I *do* think we wave it around recklessly when people are burned out and miserable as a way to say, "It's okay that you want to claw your eyes out at work because *it's for a good cause.*"

So no, #2 is not my favorite either.

My favorite reason is #3. Do brilliant work because it's one of the coolest parts of being human!

How gorgeous is it that we get to play around on the planet and try to make stuff that makes others happy? How enlivening that we can have an idea and then make that idea reality? How special is it that we can take the passion and imagination that bubbles up from the deepest parts of ourselves and share it with our fellow Earthlings?

In the most beautiful version of work I know, we're all just big kids shouting, "Hey, watch this! Look what I thought of! Look what I can do!"

Work can make us feel alive

I'm tempted to dive into a traditional Festivus airing of my grievances with busyness and conformity because, WOW, am I going to feel lighter after that. But I think we should stay with reason #3 for a beat longer: do brilliant work because it's one of the coolest parts of being human. It's *why work matters*. And more importantly, it is why *your* work matters. Choreographer Martha Graham said it best:

There is a vitality, a life force, an energy, a quickening that is translated through you into action, and because there is only one of you in all of time, this expression is unique. And if you block it, it will never exist through any other medium, and it will be lost. The world will not have it.

Friend, do you hear my voice in your head as you read this? I hope you do, because I'm sitting here in upstate NY in this Adirondack chair, trying to reach through space and time and the pages of this book to get to you to tell you this:

Work can be work, or it can be *you*.

Whether you are a marketing manager, an engineer, or a nurse, your work can be your art.

Your stamp!

Your power to decide how things should be and what would be cool.

To be part of the creation of our magical world.

Make work that wows

Me: Did you have some favorites of Milton's work? What made it brilliant?

Sue: There are two posters that I love that he did. Obviously I love "I ♥ NY," because who doesn't? But there was a poster for SVA [School of Visual Arts] that used the Magritte painting of this man with a hat and an apple in front of his face as visual inspiration and said, "Art is whatever." The "hat" [in "whatever"] was located within the image of a hat. It was the kind of thing where you just want to keep looking at it to understand what you're seeing. An image of a hat, finding "hat" in the word "whatever," and the reference to Magritte and surrealism. That's what makes it so successful. It's so interesting to look at and you can't quite find the answer, but you keep looking for it.

Have a look:

There were no limits for Milton and what he made or what he did. I think that's also what's really interesting. It wasn't like he was limited to posters or limited to being a teacher or limited to being a designer of logos, and he even designed supermarkets! One of the most surprising things that we designed together was a cork presenter for Eleven Madison Park. It was used when someone ordered a really expensive bottle of wine, and the server presented a cork as part of that experience. How do you present the cork? It was a bit random and not anything either of us had ever thought about, but despite that, it didn't feel hard. Work didn't feel hard. You didn't experience, "I can't do that"; it was always, "Oh, let's figure that out."

The barriers to brilliant work

Before we get to the "how" of doing brilliant, captivating, you-shaped work, first we need to unpack what's in the way.

Let's start with busyness and conformity as the two biggest killers of brilliant work. Also, there's a reason my autocorrect just turned "busyness" into "business," but that's an aside.

Let's take busyness first. There are four root problems that cause busyness:

1. The math problem: This is the most obvious one. Three essential things have to get done. They all take 10 minutes each. That's 30 minutes. You only have 15 minutes. So to solve this unsolvable math problem, you end up rushing through the work as fast as you can, defying that each should take 10 minutes, all while thinking, "I'm very busy!"

2. The strategy problem: You (or your business) have enough time to do the things you *need* to do, but other tasks seem to rise up out of nowhere, and you convince yourself and your fellow leaders that they need to be done, too.

Maybe one person thinks they need to be done and everyone obliges. Maybe you've all been doing these tasks for years and no one knows what would happen if you stopped doing them. Maybe the truth is that you don't have a strong, differentiated company strategy, and so instead you're trying a bunch of stuff to see what works. That's a legit strategy if you're a start-up or if you're exploring a new venture, but a bad one to pursue forever.

Regardless of what your strategy problem is, it still means you are putting 20 tasks on your company or personal plate, when that plate is one of those toddler plates that has room only for three non-touching items.

3. The power problem: In every business there are people who do the work and people who manage the work: makers versus managers. The makers' job is to produce content, code, strategies, plans, service, programs, or whatever it may be. The managers' job is to make sure that the remit of the work is in line with company strategy, that the makers understand what they're doing and have what they need, that the work is getting done well and on time, and that it's well-coordinated across other parts of the business.

Understandably, to get their jobs done, managers are constantly communicating up, down, and across the business, usually in the form of meetings and decks. The makers mostly need making time. Now, what happens when a maker's need for making time and a manager's need for status meetings collide?

Well, the person with more power wins, and that's the manager.

One way to know that this is a power problem is to notice that it doesn't exist in industries where managers have *less* power than the makers. Consider a famous singer who employs a manager. Because the maker (the artist) has the power, the making comes first. Trust me, Taylor Swift is not on Zoom calls eight hours a day.

4. The psychology problem: This ranges from a deep-seated need to feel needed all the way to existential dread. Whenever I would lead two project teams at the same time, the program manager of each project, me, and my EA would have a Slack channel that someone would name "Team Bree" so we could coordinate what meetings I should be at when. I won't lie, I felt like a fucking celebrity. My ego was dancing. I was SO VERY BUSY because I was SO VERY NEEDED. My shoulders were raw from all that brushing.

In those times I was *pulled* into being busy, but sometimes we *push* ourselves into busyness as well, usually to stay in the safe world of check-lists and away from the hard, uncertain, more meaningful work (or the rest of life). We do some version of checklist masturbation telling ourselves it's all so urgent, when in fact we *should* be attending to the important.

Brilliance requires spaciousness. But busyness's job description is to stamp out all spaciousness. Busyness is fight or flight, while brilliance is sitting in the meadow dreaming about your innovative new shelter design.

Your body is just not going to let you think about chimney design when the bear is chasing you. And it's not going to let you think about beautiful new solves to your business challenge when you have two minutes until your next meeting and you're bursting for a bathroom break. Your body is like, "We're under attack! Why else wouldn't we pee for five hours?"

Normal work is never brilliant

Okay conformity, your turn.

The pressure to produce normal-looking work is strong. Especially when we feel insecure about our work, it can feel like the safest thing to do is to make our work look like everyone else's work. This is why we get so many soul-sucking slide decks. There are the bullets and the graphs, and some-times you just look at them and say, "What is this actually saying? Is there anything interesting or profound or actionable here at all? Can you just say in a sentence what the point is and skip all the tables?" I mean, usually I say that way nicer, but that's how it goes in my head.

A lot of this comes down to *creative confidence*: the ability to create something you believe in and show it or say it clearly to others.

Take the acclaimed and definitely not normal screenwriter Stanley Kubrick. Someone once asked him if it was usual for a director to spend so much time lighting each shot. He said, "I don't know. I've never seen anyone else light a film."

The guy gave zero fucks about what normal looked like. He had confidence to do what he thought was best. Working this way honors our instincts and unrefined brilliance and liberates us from best practices. Most of all, it's brave and gives us the courage to put our ideas into the world without the safety net of "I'm just doing it how we've always done it. Don't blame me!"

In our world today, there are so many best practices and methods and frameworks that while everyone has gotten smarter, the unintended consequence has been that many things are the same. Ads for banks are the same. Billboards for sports drinks are the same. Venture capital firms—"We are investing in the next generation of world-changing companies"—are the same.

Instead, brilliant work is about having the bravery to not start with what is known, but to start with what you aren't quite sure of yet but are excited to discover, invent, and share with the world.

The value of an unspoiled mind

The only way we know if something is known or "normal" is by looking around and seeing if it matches other stuff. Conventional business thinking often begins with what is known. What do we know about the industry? Our competitors? Our customers? The economy?

But what if, when we're endeavoring to do brilliant work, we either didn't do that or looked but didn't give a shit? What if we created from an unspoiled mind? Here's what that looks like.

Unspoiled minds retain their originality

Back in my acting days, I read *Impro: Improvisation and the Theater,* which described what happens when we professionalize creativity.

A film critic told the story of what he saw time and again with film students. In their first year, each student would make a short film unaided. The films would undeniably be interesting, though technically crude. By the end of the term, students were making technically proficient films, except for the small issue that they were boring as shit. All of a sudden, everyone was much more concerned with their film appearing professional.

Every company develops a sense of "what's normal and accepted here." It's one reason why capturing your new hires within the first month or two and interviewing them is an excellent idea. At one consultancy I worked at we asked each new hire to share three things about the firm that were surprising in a good way, and three things that didn't seem to make sense, at least at first glance.

Sometimes you need an unspoiled mind to point out when you have organizational spinach in your teeth.

Unspoiled minds reject "we've always done it this way"

Have you ever heard a five-year-old ask, "Why?" to anything and everything? "Why do I have to eat with a fork? Why can't I wear a crown to school? Why can't I sleep in my fort?" They ask because they have an unspoiled, highly creative mind that doesn't accept answers at face value.

The same holds true for the world of business. If you are at a company and the answer is "because we've done it this way before and we know it works," that's a clear sign some conversations need to be had around the future of your organization.

Creative work is
not a selfish act or a
bid for attention on
the part of an actor.
It's a gift to
the world and every
being in it.

STEVEN PRESSFIELD

Other answers like "you're just a junior employee" or "you haven't been here long enough to know" are similar neon signs for conversations. All these phrases reveal a status quo has been established and cemented—and innovation is going to require breaking it up.

Unspoiled minds learn to trust their intuition over time

I'm not making the case to be reckless with your career or organization, but the more you test the waters with bold new ideas (and learn that rarely does anything truly bad happen when prototyping something new), the more likely you'll be to trust your instincts about when to stick with the tried and true and when to say, "I think there's a better way. Shall we give it a go?"

We're so often looking to others around us, we forget to look to ourselves. Cal Newport, author of *Digital Minimalism*, calls this "Solitude Deprivation: A state in which you spend close to zero time alone with your own thoughts and free from input from other minds."

Can we even hear our own instincts over the trend reports?

Although sticking with the tried-and-true option feels safer, the irony is that it's usually the people who allow themselves the freedom of original thinking who end up sticking out from the performance review calibration crowd, get promoted and put themselves in leadership positions, and, most importantly of all, *do brilliant work*.

All because they gave themselves permission.

Brilliance loves absurdity: The bakery

This is perhaps my favorite Milton story.
....

Sue: Once we were contracted to work with a pharmaceutical company that had a huge corporate campus full of all these "starchitect" buildings [buildings designed by famous architects]. They asked us to work on a wayfinding system for the buses that carry people around the campus. We met with a wayfinding design firm because we weren't specialists in wayfinding, but that never prevented Milton from working on anything. We met with the clients to learn more.

And then one day, after a weekend (sometimes you didn't know what happened in his brain over the weekend), Milton walked in and said, "We're working on the wrong project for them." And I said, "What do you mean? What's the right project for them?"

"This isn't what those people need," he said. "They don't need a signage system. They don't need a wayfinding system. They need a bakery. A bakery that would give them freshly baked bread on their way home every night. The most delicious bread ever baked."

"Okay…" I hesitated, because you know I'm thinking of the client and what they asked for, and I'm trying to figure out a way to bring them along in this decision-making… and he said, "I sketched it out." Milton had drawn up a bakery in the shape of a cake. I think he was imagining it would be this imaginative, unique space that people would go to on this very professional campus with professional, corporate buildings with professional architects. People would see the bakery, in the shape of a cake, and feel some kind of delight or joy or playfulness.

His imagination didn't have constraints… He was just thinking, "How do you improve their lives in a way that is more sensory and less practical than a wayfinding system?" He thought the feeling of eating a delicious, warm piece of bread is a feeling that everyone should have at the end of the day, and that's where he was coming from. I really loved that about him. The client was originally asking to solve for a functional need, and Milton responded by addressing the emotional experience of work to remind people life was about more than being practical.

....

I know people need signage systems. But if I worked on that campus, I'd happily get lost daily to go home with some freshly baked bread. I'm imagining that in Milton's head, Maslow's hierarchy of needs for those research scientists went 1) bread, 2) wayfinding. He may not have objected to the wayfinding project in general, but he saw a way to get at the more essential, human, life-affirming need first: the need for fresh bread.

(You have no idea how much I wanted to fit a baguette in this book for you instead of that wayfinding section up front, but the distribution team was not down with crumbs.)

When businesses talk back-to-basics and fundamentals, I think of this story. Maybe business fundamentals don't consist of tight operating processes or even company purpose. Maybe the first business fundamental should be that all employees have delicious, fresh bread. And once we're all feeling fed and happy, then we can get down to business.

It reminds me of the line in the Lord's Prayer, "Give us this day our daily bread," as a way to ask for the basics of day-to-day sustenance. No one's asking, "Give us this day our daily wayfinding system."

I love this story because at first glance it is entirely absurd. If I had a client come to me for culture work and I said, "Let me call a great baker I know!" I don't know that I'd hear back from them. But also, sometimes the most absurd ideas are the ones we need the most.

And finally, don't you think people would end up saying, "It's easy to get to the biotech building—just turn left at the cake bakery"?

Genius can exist in everyday business

Maybe it's time to distinguish between capital G genius and lowercase g genius.

I see your point that if you had all these lawless geniuses running around your business, nothing would get done and they'd probably keep breaking stuff. There would be no signage systems, and Stanley Kubrick would not be a fan of getting his expense reports done on time.

Your capital G geniuses are your internal Milton Glasers and Stanley Kubricks. Every organization needs a few of them. They're commonly found leading creative or innovation functions. As for your lowercase g geniuses, they can be everyone! Literally everyone. And I argue that that's what you *want*.

Your lowercase g geniuses do every important task with brilliance and care. This isn't just design-y creative work. I've seen genius project time-lines, genius research insights, genius facilitation of a collaboration session. They also know when to not waste their efforts on shit that just needs to get done, or on first drafts that should be messy to invite collaboration. You only want to use your genius when you're going to get great return on the time you put into it. Or in Tim Ferriss's words, "Doing something unimportant well does not make it important."

When important work is less than genius, do you know what happens? The project timing gets screwed and everyone's busy and working late to catch up. The team ends up producing crappy ideas, based on crappy insights, and the work itself becomes crappy. And the people in that collaboration session end up misunderstanding each other, and resentment brews. The price of not prioritizing genius is more busyness, which leaves even less room for genius. It's a downward spiral.

Who is doing the brilliant thinking and when?

When I first started in consulting, I remember being shocked that not all, but a *lot* of CEOs were not coming up with the company strategy. Instead, this is frequently done by a strategy team or some task force of senior leadership that puts together data and recommendations and likely facilitates a workshop. And then the CEO and the rest of the executive leadership team will ingest the recommendations and be like, "Option #3, please." Or there's a prioritization exercise and 17 things end up prioritized and then the more junior team has to figure out who's going to do all of those 17 things and everyone suddenly gets very busy.

In fact, that strategy team was already busy leading up to that workshop, so they didn't have the time or space to do truly brilliant strategic thinking to create the input. The leadership team has probably allotted four hours of a day and a half offsite sitting in some windowless hotel ballroom, so *they're* not doing the truly brilliant strategic thinking.

So *who fucking is*?!

You'd hope that at the very least there's room for brilliant execution, but for all those people who are running around executing on the 17 things, I guarantee you a third to a half of their time is taken up reporting back with status updates in fancy decks shown in fancy meetings. When leaders expect their team to come with brilliant input and the team expects leaders to come with brilliant vision, but everyone is too busy to do either, well, then, the brilliance never comes. (I suppose that's why they hire consultants, so perhaps I should keep my mouth shut on this one!)

As much as I want to keep selling more consulting work so I can hang out with Sue and Huma and Jacques and all the rest, I also believe everyone would be happier (leaders, employees, the world!) if people were regularly protecting their own time and space to simply *think*.

We make ourselves busy and normal

Who decided that we should run around looking busy and normal, when no one really wants to?

According to Dorie Clark in *Harvard Business Review*, "97 percent of leaders say long-term thinking is critical, and 96 percent of leaders say they don't have time for it."

And according to *Fortune*, "Employees spend 32 percent of their time on average dedicated to performative tasks that don't directly contribute to their company's goals. That's approximately 12.8 hours of a 40-hour work week. The reason? Many workers point to the hyper-focus among higher-ups on employee output and the feeling that they always need to be on."

So the leaders don't like it. The employees don't like it. And customers and shareholders can't particularly like it because busywork is leaking organizational fuel that's not contributing to the impact or success of the company. WTF?

What will it take for us to do less? To give ourselves time and permission to be healthy and brilliant? To do the important, scary work?

Outside of the ER, most urgency is made up—*by us*. We decide to do quarterly business reviews, to set internal deadlines, and to promise 24-hour turnarounds on who knows what. Sure, sometimes these things are helpful forcing functions, but more often we make ourselves crazy with them, and the amount of *actually* brilliant work we do suffers because of it.

Perhaps a good analogy here is when one kid takes another kid's hand and smacks it into that other kid's head saying, "Why are you hitting yourself?" Except we are hitting ourselves, and, *yes, we look that stupid* . . . it's corporate masochism.

Can we not?

Meet the boss of work

Bob is back on Earth, and his mission this time is to figure out who the boss is. "Easy one!" he thinks.

It's Google Calendar.

Bob writes in his report: "The humans are chronically tired and don't even eat or go to the bathroom when they need to. They just go where the almighty Google Calendar tells them to go."

And he wouldn't be wrong...

HOW TO DO LESS, BETTER WORK

Amuse yourself

In figuring out how to do less, better work, I prefer a "crowd it out" strategy. It's much easier to first figure out the brilliant, important work we should be doing, start getting into it, and then just let all that other stuff casually slide off the list of priorities.

Which leads to this question: How do we know what the brilliant, important work is that we should focus on?

There are a few ways to answer this question, and, yes, I have a few favorites. It's tricky because I want to address this question at two levels: the individual level of what's brilliant, important work for you personally; and the team and organizational level of what's brilliant, important work for the whole.

Let's start with you.

When Marc and I are creating a new business proposal, typically we have an initial conversation with a potential client, and then we debrief to figure out what work we want to propose. We talk about the client, their business context, their stated (and potential unstated) needs, their appetite for the work, and a host of other considerations. And then invariably we stop to look at each other. And one of us asks, "What work would be the most *fun* to do?" Usually that's the work we end up proposing!

Maybe you're reading this in shock because it sounds like we're taking our client's money to entertain ourselves. Well, that's only partially true. Marc and I both have little patience for busyness and conformity. We know that what the client wants—what they're paying us the big bucks for—is brilliant work. So to hell with all of the normal-looking strategy presentations. We propose the work that we know will light us up and will light a team up. Rick Rubin, author of *The Creative Act*, says it well: "The best work is the work you are excited about."

So option one: you follow your excitement to brilliant, important work.

Or option two: you use your fear as a compass.

Steven Pressfield, author of *The War of Art*, has a rule of thumb to use when you find yourself possessed by resistance that stops you from doing your most brilliant work: "The more scared we are of a work or calling, the more sure we can be that we have to do it."

Sure, doing what you fear most sometimes lends itself to things like quitting your job and trying to make it as an actor in LA. (I did this exact thing when I was 23, and although I failed miserably, I don't regret it!) But it also produces greatness. Businesses often struggle because they don't differentiate. They fail to be brave because the leaders are incentivized to look "normal" to their boards, and so they try to avoid anything terrible happening in their tenure.

How boring.

And also, how ineffective! What do they do instead? They take the normal route to answering the question, "What is the brilliant, important work we should focus on?" and that is called—get ready to swoon—"strategic planning." Okay, maybe I'm being a little spicy here.

I do support attention to strategy, planning, prioritization. I support a comprehensive look around the business for the different forces at play, from what's happening in the industry, to what's happening in technology and culture, what's happening with customers, competitors, employees, and all the rest. It's all good. It's just not enough. It's missing the best part:

What you actually want to do!

I don't know how this happens, but somewhere along the way of organizational maturity, everyone stops believing they have the agency to choose what's fun, enlivening, and brilliant.

Employees figure they have to wait for leadership to come up with the vision and then do that. Leaders seem to think their main job is to keep the business steady and responsive to the board, shareholders, customers, and anyone else leaders think of as their boss. Honestly, over the course of my consulting career, it has shocked me how many leaders feel some combination of trapped, stuck, and needing to please their many stakeholders before ever considering their own vision.

This is a miss.

You get to decide what excites you. Yes, YOU. You get a say! Your team wants you to have a say, as do customers, Wall Street, and everyone else, because it ACTUALLY MAKES BETTER WORK.

Amuse yourself, please!

Revere your ideas

Me: What sort of things excited Milton most?

Sue: You know, I would go into work, and sometimes you just didn't know what was going to happen that day. We would have things to do for clients, but that might not be what Milton found important that day. There was never this sense of beholdenness with him to clients or expectations. Of course, we would do the work we needed to do, but not always in the way that you would in a "professional" setting.

One day I walked in and he said, "I have an idea. I think that we should make a beautiful glass." I saw that he had already sketched it and said, "Okay, say more... what are you talking about?" And he said, "I think everyone in the world should get this glass—" in his mind I think it was made of crystal "—and take a cool drink of water from the glass at the same time."

I thought of the global population—8 billion people. Eight billion glasses.

"Wait," I said. "How would we even do that?"

And he replied, "That doesn't really matter... we'll figure it out."

I said, "Milton, how would we even get everyone on this block—on 32nd street—to drink a glass of water at the same time, let alone everyone, like, people in Mongolia and Antarctica and people in the desert?" The logistics really stopped me. I kept thinking of the impossibility of this idea. Milton, however, wasn't interested in that kind of thing.

What I love about this idea now is that it wasn't balanced by logic, and it wasn't tempered by the assumptions of what we thought we could or couldn't do. Realistically speaking, there's no way we could have really done that. But Milton was coming from a place of "How do we have a communal and beautiful experience with each other?" and that's a really amazing thing. That is so important. How do we create shared experiences of humanity?

Why isn't there more imagination? Ideas that aren't bound to what we know we can and can't do, you know? A lot of times ideas have a fragility because they're going to rub up against all the things that make things not happen. There are the logistics, the priorities, the resources, the workplans, the budget… all of the things that exist in a professional environment. There are always reasons to not move forward with an idea.

With Milton, the ideas were never fragile. The ideas were the important thing, the most important thing.

Know your muse

Maybe you know what it is that excites you and/or spins you around in fear. If so, carry on!

But perhaps I shouldn't skip the part about generating those enlivening ideas in the first place. Truly brilliant ideas, in my experience, show up when they want to, like Taylor Swift's sparkly cloud. But the most creative people I know don't just wait for their muse. They prepare for her and learn her ways. Hat tip to Steven Pressfield, who first inspired me to see the capital *M* Muse in all her glory.

- The Muse loves cozy teams who say what they think. She gets annoyed if she blesses a team member with a brilliant thought and they keep it to themselves because they deem it "not normal."

- She hates 30-minute meetings. She doesn't even participate. She just watches, laughing at the humans who are trying to substitute efficiency for brilliance. In the words of Ed Catmull, former Pixar president, "The goal isn't efficiency; it is to make something good or even great."

- She loves movement. Friedrich Nietzsche tells us, "Only those thoughts that come by walking have any value." Stanford researchers found that a person's creative output increases by an average of 60 percent while walking as compared with sitting.

- She really loves showers, and especially when you shampoo your hair. She highly recommends you get one of those waterproof notepads that stick to your shower walls, because she's not going to bless you again 20 minutes later when you're at your desk trying to remember her inspiration.

- She loves a powerhouse, someone with a tad too much audacity. If she's going to go to the trouble of inspiring you, she wants to see her ideas executed.

- She hates grumpy, tired people. They're no good at listening or making anything happen.

- She hates busy people, too. The Muse will not be "back-burnered."

- She thinks it's cute when you're excited. She considers your "Ooh! What if we...?" exclamations as flirtation.

- She hates the song "Luck Be a Lady" because she's mistaken for luck far too often, and the Muse is an entirely different, singular deity not to be confused with anyone.

- And she does love an offsite or, even better, a Do Nothing Day.

Sit and think

I adore Agatha Christie novels, and particularly Hercule Poirot mysteries. The fictional detective is famous for eschewing typical methods, such as crawling on the ground looking for stray scraps of evidence. To him, the running around, interviews, and forensics are better done by the police who have their routines. Instead, he claims, "It is enough for me to sit back in my chair and think."

Just sit.

And think.

A few years ago, I was leading a project in which we were designing an immersive company-wide experience for employees. We knew the work needed to be strategic and brilliantly executed, but most of all, it needed to be captivating.

But captivating is rarely conjured in a 60-minute brainstorm session. Our brains struggle to produce truly audacious thinking when we're distracted by the meeting after this one, wondering when we're going to refill our coffee, and seeing Slack, email, and text pop-ups. With so many distractions, our brains are working to *reduce* the noise: return the text, delete the email, snooze the alert. But creativity requires *creating* noise: dreaming up messiness, noticing the funny wrinkles, letting 73 bad ideas flush from our brains before the brilliant #74 comes.

With this in mind, Sue and I devised what we call a "Do Nothing Day." The trick is you have to tell yourself you don't have to produce *anything*. For a whole day. And you have to be legit okay with that if you're the leader or PM.

Still, even though the whole point was to be okay with the day *not* delivering, it sure did. The best idea the team came up with that day ended up being the highest-rated component of the entire experience BY FAR. That idea was in us; it just needed time and space to find its way out.

Have a Do Nothing Day

Maybe you're thinking, "But how do you *do* a DND? As in, how do I plan one of these and get away with it? Do I have to call it a 'Do Nothing Day' on my public work calendar?"

First, as for what to call it on your calendar, it's tough. You must commit to telling yourself it's a Do Nothing Day. And you honestly have to be okay if nothing comes of it. But if it makes life easier to tell others it's a "Brainstorming Day" or "Ideation Block" or "Very Business-y Productivity Day," then by all means. Just don't go promising a colleague or client a report of brilliant ideas.

Next, let me be clear about what a DND is and what it is not, because I know the name is confusing. I hear this a lot: "Schedule a Do Nothing Day? Impossible! With our deadlines, we need more do *everything* days!"

A DND is:

- A working day. It is a productive day, just not in the way we normally think about productivity. It's a day of thinking and visioning without making anything.
- An antidote to working hard on the wrong stuff. In any team or organization, if the *thinking* is not sound, the *execution* will be crap. Aren't your months of sprinting and late nights worth one day of asking, "Is there something we should be doing instead? What haven't we thought of? What's a more elegant solve here? What would make for more captivating work?"

A DND is not:

- Paid time off
- A day for the team to go to a museum for inspiration (a good thing! just different)
- A teambuilding day (I mean, it can feel like bonding, but that's not the goal)

To see takes time.

GEORGIA O'KEEFFE

The DND strategy

There is too little respect for thinking (as in the *act* of thinking) in business today. Trust me, Van Gogh was never like, "Okay, I have 30 minutes until my paint supplier status meeting. Better knock out a painting."

A DND is a way to protect the time and space our brains need in order to wander, explore, dream, debate, and conjure. Every single time I've led a proper, day-long DND (and it doesn't escape me it's the same acronym as for "do not disturb"), we have come up with one or more ideas that have contributed *massively* to the success of our project.

But here's the thing: you have to woo the Muse. She does not like impatience and she doesn't respond to pressure. Ever tried starting a brainstorm meeting with "Okay team, give me your best five ideas. Go!"? No, you must lay down the picnic blanket, invite the Muse to tea, and tell her, "No hurry, we have all day!" Only then might she decide to join you.

Before I give you the how-to, here are some things you will need to gather and prepare for your DND.

One of your main tools will be two sets of card prompts:

Deck A: Each card should have a different topic related to your project/work. For our DND on an employee-wide experience, our card topics were "the opening," "session on customers," "session on culture," and "leadership profiles." You need a basic framework of five to seven prompts to give the day momentum.

Deck B: These cards are just for fun and to delight the Muse. If you're feeling creative, you can come up with your own prompts. Some classic ones are "How would Oprah approach the opportunity?" and "What if you had to solve your challenge in five minutes?" You might also try the Oblique Strategies deck created by Brian Eno and Peter Schmidt for their own work as artists and musicians, with classic prompts such as "The most important thing is the most easily forgotten" and "Abandon normal instruments."

More practically, you will need:

- Mini portable dry erase boards with markers, one per person
- Blankets to sit on if you're going to a park
- Snacks! Or make sure you're near somewhere to get food/drinks

Now, let's get to the how-to:

Define the scope: What is the focus of your Do Nothing Day? It could be ideas for a project, or new revenue opportunities or internal operational improvements, or a five-year company vision.

Block off the time: Make it a day. The Muse is not impressed with your half-day effort. I mean, you can try if you want, and maybe it's better than nothing, but if you half-ass it, so will the Muse.

Pick a non-worklike location: Ideally your DND is held in person and away from your office. I wouldn't recommend even trying a virtual DND. Not worth the investment. It can be in your office if it's a must, but the Muse is much more impressed if you bring her to a green space, or at least a room with a view. Under no circumstances should you choose a windowless hotel ballroom. The Muse will flat out refuse to attend.

Set the intention: Say something like "Today is about [your scope]. This is a day to think about EVERYTHING and do NOTHING. So I say to all of your brains: YOU ARE FREE! You don't have to do anything. Nothing to make or email or Slack. Just play. If nothing comes of this day, no biggie! We planned for that."

Use the cards as needed: Start with a card from Deck A and invite people to dream. You can walk, sit in the grass, eat fried chicken, take a nap, go down rabbit holes. The mini white boards are nice if everyone is feeling contemplative and wants to scatter and write/sketch their own thoughts. When you feel like it, you can come together and each share your thoughts. No time boxing. If one person's thought strikes the group's interest, then hang around there as long as you like. When momentum slows, either stay on the same topic from Deck A and use Deck B for fresh inspiration, or move on to a new card from Deck A. You may spend 30 minutes on one Deck A card, or 3 hours.

Let your excitement guide you: If a conversation is boring, stop having it! If you feel excitement starting to buzz and catch the faint whiff of the Muse's perfume, don't stop!

Capture some of your ideas: Photos of your white boards is sufficient. You definitely don't need a full-on notetaker. But if one person is looking out for the ideas that get everyone excited and jots them down, you'll thank yourself later.

Go out to a team dinner! For whomever can join. Enjoy each other.

If you have any lingering doubts about whether this is a legit way to spend a day of work, a gentle reminder: If you are a knowledge worker, thinking *is* working. It is in fact your job.

Design brilliance into your day-to-day

Like many people, I've fallen for the allure of waking at 5 am and going for a run and churning out my first brilliant idea before 7 am. In theory, anyway. Problem is, I hate getting up that early. I also hate running. Fortunately, there are simple ways to delight your muse during working hours. I invite you to jot down what you might do.

Move your rocks. If every time you go for a walk in the woods there's a rock in your way, maybe you walk around the rock the first two times. By the third time, it's time to move that rock! The Muse has no patience for resetting passwords, unintuitive document-naming conventions, or missing power cords.

The one rock I will move today:

Try a 10-minute workday. Every morning, pretend you have only 10 minutes to work that day. What would you do? Instinctively, you're likely to pick the most valuable task and/or the task that only you could do given your knowledge, expertise, connections, or other unique asset. When you know that thing, start your day with it and give it everything you've got (even if it secretly takes you more than 10 minutes). One CEO I worked with did this every morning, and once she decided her thing for the day, she wrote it down at the top of her calendar. Any subsequent meetings or tasks for the day were evaluated against it, as in, "Is it helping me achieve my one thing, or not?"

My #1 task for today:

Arrive early. To everything. I say this one like it's something I do, but I can assure you I at least try. Why? Because all the best things happen in the slack—that unaccounted for time between the appointments of our day. The unoptimized slack is when I remember to text my colleague who was out and see how she's feeling. It's when I remember that we know our client's favorite dessert and decide that's what we should have as a snack during the offsite. It's when I suddenly know what I should write about next. The Muse delights in unoptimized slack and frequently visits me there.

The next place I'm going to arrive to 10 minutes early:

Move. If you are sitting at a desk in front of a computer for eight hours a day, the Muse will roll her eyes at you. If you find yourself stuck, instead of hunkering down and trying harder, go for a walk, do 10 burpees, stretch, or find a window to open and stick your head out of it. The Muse just might pity you enough to oblige.

What I'll do the next time I'm stuck:

```



```

Remember you're an outdoor cat. In computer science, "garbage in, garbage out" (GIGO) means the output of a model is only as good as the data you put into it. Same for your brain. To do inspiring work, you first have to feel inspired! This can mean going to museums or lectures, taking yourself on walks in the woods, or making it a practice to invite interesting people to coffee to swap stories. Roam free and explore!

The next place I'm foraging for inspiration:

```



```

Closing thought, from Milton

Sue: The front door of the building that Milton owned said "Art Is Work," and that was a meaningful way to come into work every day.

Me: I was curious about that saying, because I could interpret it either as "Art shouldn't be thought of as fanciful or silly; it's really important work" or "Art is hard," in the way you would say, "Art is WORK."

Sue: It was more of the first. It's meaningful and important and sometimes it feels hard, but Milton never made it seem like it felt that hard. He would just start working; he would just start making something. People would always ask, "What's your process?" and he didn't understand why people asked that, or where they were coming from. He would always say, "You just start working." Start sketching, messing around, let ideas come to you. It was mysterious to him that there was any alternative to that.

5

KEEP IT COOL— WE'RE ALL IN IT TOGETHER

Astonishingly, work is not all fun and games and DNDs. There will always be some amount of stress present. Someone does something stupid that sets you back or you find yourself with too short a deadline, or a customer or client is upset. I could fill a chapter with reasons we get stressed at work. The question is, What do we do when those things inevitably happen? How do we manage our own emotions and experience? How do we show up for our team?

I've talked a lot about how to ride the high of fun, humanity, camaraderie, and brilliant work, but it's worth a chapter to talk about what we do with the lows. Because you know what is decidedly *not* fun? Managing someone else's emotions.

If you've had a volatile parent, dated someone mercurial, or been parent to a toddler or teenager, you'll know that it's fucking exhausting. Nobody likes it. So the best thing we can do as leaders and colleagues is not be that volatile person to others. Consider this quote from an employee I spoke to when supporting one client with their culture:

We work in an extraordinarily chaotic environment. Managers need to really role model calmness . . . a predictability of response when people come to say, "Hey, I think I have a problem and I need some help." They need to know that their manager is not going to lose the plot and go crazy. That kind of calmness is crucial.

There are two main benefits to being a cool-headed leader:

1 **Not sucking:** A stressed-out, anxiety-producing leader makes a team culture categorically suck, no matter how good everything else is. Business can be good, the work can be interesting, and the pay can be excellent, but if your leader is wound up and leaking their stress everywhere, I guarantee that team is not joyful. The only exception might be when the team is bonding over their hatred of said leader. Note: This is no leader's ideal team bonding plan.

2 **Being brilliant and fun:** Being cool-headed not only makes you not suck, but it makes you sturdy enough to handle whatever the business throws at you with grace and wisdom. It helps you make sound, thoughtful decisions. It helps you be able to take work seriously; but yourself, not so much. And what am I saying? It helps you take work not that seriously either. One of my all-time favorite clients, Melisa Goldie, used to say when she was the CMO of Calvin Klein, "Look, people, we're not saving lives. There's no such thing as a fashion emergency." It's true, even if Arden debates me on this point.

I'll dive into both these benefits in this chapter.

IN THIS CHAPTER

THE MOST UNDERRATED LEADERSHIP SKILL IS EMOTIONAL RELIABILITY

Fun requires emotional reliability

I wanted to open the book with the simple belief that work should be fun, but in many ways, this chapter is the prerequisite to chapter 1. As I shared earlier, if a leader is spewing stress all over the place, a ping pong table is *definitely* not going to fix it.

Psychologist Dr. Becky Kennedy, author of the parenting book *Good Inside*, says that "the wider range of feelings we can regulate—if we can manage the frustration, disappointment, envy, and sadness—the more space we have to cultivate happiness... Regulation first, happiness second."

Yes, she's speaking about parenting, but I dare say learning to skillfully regulate our own emotions takes a lifetime.

Emotionally reliable leaders do three things

I've worked with many leaders over the years, and one thing that always surprises me is how many don't internalize their own power. They spend their entire careers reaching for authority, only to forget its influence once they have it.

For example, I've seen many leaders mention, just in passing, a nascent idea, and unbeknownst to them their team scrambles to execute on it as a directive. Similarly, I've seen many senior leaders self-conceive as "middle management" in the grand scheme of a large organization, when they might as well be the CEO to their team. Like the Great Dane trying to sit in his owner's lap, leaders don't always know their own weight. Whether this is true for you is something only you can answer. But I suspect that whatever power you feel you have, your team thinks you have more.

One of the most important qualities a leader can foster (in themselves and the broader workplace) is the trust that they can be emotionally reliable. It's what gives employees and team members the confidence to speak openly with their managers, VPs, and executives and know these individuals (in positions of authority) will keep their cool in moments of crisis, stress, or instability. Don't get me wrong—I am not arguing that leaders need to suppress their emotions. Emotionally reliable leaders can be *highly* emotive. They simply know how to process and communicate their emotions in a healthy way such that their emotions don't get the best of them.

Here are a few ways emotionally reliable leaders foster this sort of trust with their teammates.

Emotionally reliable leaders don't "leak" their feelings

Many leaders don't internalize how a flash of frustration on their face or an exasperated sigh is immediately picked up by their teams.

These cues give individuals insight into how the leader (whom they likely do not interact with as often as their own peers and coworkers) feels about a given situation. In some cases, these cues are more important than the words the leader uses. They're a more authentic glimpse into what the individual is feeling, not just thinking.

Behavioral psychologist Dr. Albert Mehrabian showed that only 7 percent of communication occurs through verbal expression, while 38 percent of information shows up in your tone of voice, and a whopping 55 percent is expressed through body language. That means, even when a leader feels like they are keeping it together and saying the right things, their voice and body are likely betraying them. When leaders are not processing their own emotions and sharing their emotions in a healthy way with their team, their team is likely drawing their own conclusions about the stress signals they see: "Is it me? Did I do something wrong? Is our team headed for a crisis?"

Emotionally reliable leaders are self-aware

CEOs have bad days. Managers aren't perfect. Maybe they're having a bad day because something happened with a friend or family member. Maybe they're stressed about moving or the fact they had to cancel an upcoming vacation.

Emotionally reliable leaders know why they're feeling what they're feeling and share it with their team. They have the self-awareness to say, "I am feeling a lot of anxiety right now because of this big move, and I am working through that. It's not the project. I just wanted you all to know. Team, you are doing great."

This level of transparency goes against everything the legacy business world believes about professionalism, often another word for suppressed emotion. But in reality, transparency models healthy behavior. It gives team members the permission to bring empathy into the workplace, which leads to better emotional responses all round.

Emotionally reliable leaders have a non-anxious presence

I have always liked the term "a non-anxious presence," a concept originally coined by the family therapist Edwin Friedman.

There will always be anxiety in life and in business. Success isn't about not feeling the anxiety. It's about how you express it, how you model working through it, and how you make clear the source of that anxiety.

Emotionally reliable leaders communicate how they are feeling and the source of those feelings. For example, if you are feeling anxious about an upcoming project deliverable, you may say to your team, "Hey, everyone, I was feeling a bit anxious this past weekend about the fact that we're behind schedule. Let's work together today to get caught up so that we can all feel good about this product launch on Friday." You can immediately tell how much more productive and healthy that form of communication would be for a team—as opposed to you huffing and puffing your way through the day, not vocalizing how you're feeling or why.

Ironically, being a non-anxious presence does not mean being void of anxiety. It means creating a team culture where anxiety isn't crippling and isn't personal. It's simply a part of being human and something a team can help each other get through—together.

Your emotions are contagious

Have you ever been in a meeting where everyone was very serious and you were like, "Oh yes, I will use my serious voice too. Very official business"? Contrast that meeting to the one where the highest-power individual in the meeting was laughing and chomping on a sandwich. When I'm in these scenarios, despite being a grown-up with a strong sense of self, I still feel an unspoken pressure to match the mood of the group. And after a while of speaking in my most business-y voice, you know what? I'm not faking it; my mood actually *is* more in line with the group.

When we talk about culture, sometimes we think of values and behaviors or processes and rituals, or a whole host of other facets of an organization or team. But sometimes what makes the biggest difference— a disproportionately large difference—is emotional contagion, or the transfer of moods among people in a group.

What does this mean for you if you hold power in a group? You are Typhoid Mary, my friend.

Psychologist Dr. Haim Ginott said it well: "I have come to a frightening conclusion. I am the decisive element . . . It is my personal approach that creates the climate. It is my daily mood that makes the weather." So if you're feeling all sorts of feelings about the business or the team or the work, here's what you do:

You tell the truth.

If you're grumpy, you can say, "I'm grumpy today." It's far superior to *acting* grumpy and having the whole team wondering why.

If you are excited about the future of the business or team or project, say so! If you are worried about the financial state of the business, you should say that, too! If you're a leader, I'm going to assume you always have some degree of hope for your team or the organization, even when times are rough. (If you don't, I recommend sprucing up that résumé.) So if you're going to share worry, the trick is to share it with hope as a combo deal. Not as a spin to the hard truth, but because you *do* have hope and, even better, a path forward. That's the job of a leader.

Sometimes I get the question, "Can a leader be *too* chill?" And the answer is YES. If you give off "we've got it behind closed doors" vibes, you're risking people's connection to the business and making them believe you don't trust them to be part of the solution.

If you need your people to rally together and whip out some heroics for the team or business, then you need to gameplan together, point to the hill you're taking, and shout, "We ride at dawn!"

Remember, if you're following child labor laws, your people are grown-ass adults who not only can handle the hard times but also want to be part of the path to better times. Tell the truth; invite them in!

Don't eliminate your emotions, domesticate them

Although I did title this chapter "Keep It Cool," you can probably tell by now it's not about being emotionless. Neither is it the equivalent of bickering with someone and them telling you to RELAX, which is the single stupidest thing anyone could say in that situation.

It's not about suppressing, ignoring, or shaming yourself for having feelings. Instead, it's about being really fucking masterful at knowing what to do with them. Which is the definition of Stoicism, if you ask me. As Nassim Taleb says, "Stoicism is about the domestication of emotions, not their elimination."

When people ask me how I managed through the months of caregiving for my mother with a terminal cancer diagnosis, along with caring for my father with Alzheimer's, I tell them I found three sources of magic:

1 **Anti-anxiety medication:** I was happy to receive all the brain chemistry help I could get.

2 **Stoicism:** Understanding that the ancient Stoics were generally happy people who enjoyed the pleasures of life—*despite* wars, plagues, banishments, and the death of many children—was powerful. I was not the first human to navigate a tough time, and I wouldn't be the last. I used their secrets—namely, learning to focus on what I could control.

3 **Brad:** He was incredible during that time, and my therapist gave me the advice to proactively tell him what I needed. So I told him, "Brad, can you make me a cocktail every night when I come home from the hospital and then rub my back?" And he did! I'd drink the cocktail while curled up next to him watching the greatest antidote to existential grief I know: *The Great British Bake Off*.

So I suppose I'm recommending meds, cocktails, marrying well, and British reality TV, but let's focus on the Stoic trait of emotional reliability for now.

I'm a big fan of people feeling their feelings. "The only way out is through," as they say. But sometimes what can help to shrink feelings of stress and anxiety is the delightful guilty pleasure of hearing about *other* people who are having an even *worse* time!

Want to hear a few fun stories? One about losing your life's work and one about losing a limb?

They're lessons in how to manage the emotions that come with shit happening. And even more than that, they're lessons in how you might begin to consider a hopeful perspective, as in, "Wait, could this disaster be... awesome?! Could this pile of shit be the beginning of my manure empire?"

This is what the Stoics meant by the phrase amor fati, or "love your fate." You don't just endure what comes your way, but you love it.

You use it—just like Ernest Hemingway.

People who lost their shit and didn't lose their shit: Ernest Hemingway

In 1922, Hemingway was an unpublished, struggling writer. While on extended assignment covering news events in Switzerland, he asked his wife, Hadley Richardson, to join him. It's unclear whether Hemingway asked Richardson to bring his work or she thought he'd want to work on some of it, but either way, she packed the entirety of his writing into a suitcase: manuscripts, short stories, poetry, an unfinished novel, and even the carbon copies he had made. Dun dun DUNNNN...

On a stopover at Paris's Gare de Lyon, a porter offered to take her bags to her seat, and she took the moment to buy a snack for the journey. When she got back, she found the suitcase of writing gone.

Hemingway's life work—lost in an instant.

Makes me losing my 10-page college essay when Word crashed look like small potatoes, and I'm pretty sure I cried and screamed and did not at all keep it cool.

So what did Hemingway do? Well, first he was grumpy as shit. In a letter to a friend, he wrote, "You, naturally, would say, 'Good,' etc. But don't say it to me. I ain't yet reached that mood."

We have to be patient with ourselves. It takes time to process, to feel the frustration, to allow ourselves to come around. Could you imagine if Richardson was like, "Ernest, RELAX"?

The trick is to let yourself visit the land of "woe is me" but not set up camp. The great leaders are the ones who can feel fully, process thoroughly, and move on to amoring their fati quickly. Want to know what Hemingway did?

He was like, "Fuck all that time-consuming prose. Not doing that again. I'm going to write shorter, cleaner sentences." That lean prose?

That's what he became famous for.

People who lost their shit and didn't lose their shit: My mom

If you were to say to me, "Maybe your mom's cancer diagnosis is lucky!" I would punch you in the face. Or I'd want to, anyway, since I don't know how to punch. So let me be clear, no one wants to be told, "It's not all that bad!" That's just mean and invalidating. The only way to get there, to that frame of mind, is to go yourself. If you were to tell me about something awful that happened at work, I would 100 percent say, "That happened?! That sounds terrible! Tell me more."

The nine months I spent with my mom were excruciating in many ways, but also pretty fun! I've lived away from my parents my entire adult life, seeing them about three times a year for a few days at most. In all likelihood, it would have been that way forever.

So imagine my mom lived another 20 years, to 93. That's 20 years times 3 visits per year times (generously) 4 days, which gives me 240 more days I would have seen my mom. I took care of her for nine months, from diagnosis to her passing, seeing her 98 percent of those days: 9 months times 30 days times 98 percent gives me 265 days. With that math, I consider myself a winner.

Immediately after her diagnosis (as in, within days), I moved her and my dad to NYC, got her an appointment with the head of thoracic oncology at Memorial Sloan Kettering Cancer Center (true angels those people are— Dr. Rudin, Dr. Bartelstein, Maureen, Roberta, and all the rest), and a week later, with Brad, drove their two dogs and two cats from Chicago to NYC.

I decided I had one strategy, and that was to leave all my love on the table. To hold nothing back. It was tiring, yes, but not a drain, and there's a difference. It filled me with joy and pride to be able to take time off work and give my mom my best, like she had always given me.

I knew in my bones that when I was next to my mom, that was exactly where I wanted to be. You might think we spent the time crying and having panic attacks, but it wasn't like that at all. My mom was the best Stoic I've ever known. We spent it making smoothies, walking to the park, and eating at fabulous New York restaurants with reckless abandon. Laughing at funny things my dad would say, because as sad as it is, Alzheimer's is sometimes funny. We laughed so much. Some people's parents die in car crashes and that's it. I found myself feeling gratitude that I had all this beautiful and happy time with her.

Want to hear my best amputation joke?

Right, so the chemo suppressed my mom's immune system enough for the wound on her ankle (after all those ankle surgeries) to become infected, which led to sepsis and her needing an amputation. When I first saw her after she came out of surgery, I said, "Mom, you look great! Did you lose weight?"

We laughed and laughed, amoring the fati.

Your free-to-use let's-keep-it-all-in-perspective meeting agenda:

1 We're all going to die and none of this will matter

2 Project status updates

If you keep it cool, you can stay in the fire

Ha, right, I almost forgot this was a book about work. What does this kind of emotional reliability, resilience, and love of fate look like in practice, in the office?

One of my favorite clients told me a story about some feedback he had received. He was proposing brave new ideas for the organization and trying to make them stick, but ultimately found himself pulling back when he sensed resistance or complexity. A colleague told him, "You know what you have to do, right? You have to stay in the fire longer." She meant that it would be his ability to stay with and work through complexities that come with change that would eventually make him successful.

Perhaps you're thinking, "Ha! When am I not in the fire?" What we know for sure is there will always be challenges, troubles, and complexity in leadership. The question is whether you can turn that friction into fuel. Like those deep-sea creatures that survive on carbon from thermal vents.

Some of the greatest leaders I know are great *precisely* because they can survive in habitats uninhabitable to most. They can keep the faith and the north star, work through resistance with empathy and grace, and continue to pace themselves while they do so. Notably, these exotic leadership creatures are not just grinning-and-bearing the complexity, they're living off it! Finding fun and challenge in it.

Optimism in the face of shit

At one executive leadership summit I was facilitating, the CEO shared a joke that represented his long-held principles of resilience and optimism (or in other words, emotional reliability and amor fatiness). Want to hear it?

A psychologist wanted to learn about optimism and pessimism in children, and so she brought in two kids for an experiment. She put one in a room with a big pile of toys and the other in a room with a big pile of horse shit.

After an hour, she checked on the kid with the toys. He was crying in the corner and said, "None of these are good toys!" She then checked on the kid with the horse shit. Much to her surprise, the kid was neck-deep in the shit, digging with a huge smile on his face. "What on earth are you doing?!" the psychologist asked. The kid replied, "With all this shit, there must be a pony somewhere!"

It all passes

But, Bree, you might say, what if I can't find the pony in the horseshit? What if it's just a tragedy through and through? Or a meaningless, annoying, paper cut of life? What if I'm smart enough to know a pony would not walk into a pile of his own shit?

It's said an Eastern king once asked his wisest philosophers to provide him with a sentence that would be not only true in every situation but always worth hearing, too. They presented him with these words: "And this, too, shall pass away."

As you read in the introduction, I'm a firm believer in *not* wishing away our days or enduring much of anything. Because the opposite of a bad day isn't a good day. It's *no* day. As in, would you rather try to enjoy a bad day or be dead? I'd rather the former 100 percent of the time.

And yet, perhaps there are some circumstances in which begrudging endurance is appropriate. I tend to limit them to extreme intestinal distress, dental work, and the plank position. But if you want to throw in bad earnings calls, needing to fire someone, and submitting expenses, then by all means endure away. As Marcus Aurelius tells us, "If it's endurable, then endure it." I bet he would have made a killer personal trainer.

If all else fails, when I'm having a bad day and there's just nothing more to do or say about it, I turn to a classic bit of IT guidance: Have you tried turning it off and on again?

See you in the morning!

HOW TO BE COOL

Shout: "NEVERTHELESS!"

If you're thinking, "Bree, it sounds like kind of a lot to go on this journey of emotional regulation … Can you just, like, give me something to yell that will make it better?"

I can't, but our good friend Milton can: NEVERTHELESS!
....

Sue: When I worked with Milton, he was in his eighties. During that time, many people that he knew passed away. Someone would call the studio, and often we'd be sitting so close together that I could hear what was being said, and I would assume someone had passed away. I would tell him, "Oh I'm so sorry." Milton would be quiet for a minute, and then he would say, "Nevertheless! Where were we?" And I would think, "Okay! I guess we're going back to work now." He didn't dwell on a lot. Loss affected him, of course, and he had many people that he had great relationships with throughout his life. But he would never wallow. I think work, in a way, helped him move through experiences.
....

Sue also told me that Milton would have drawn the "nevertheless" card when the city botched a remake of his I ♥ NY campaign in 2023 with an updated "We ♥ NYC" logo.
....

Sue: The remake was so bad, and you could tell it was designed by probably 40 agencies, no real point of view, it was just bland and pretty terrible. It wasn't successful. People revolted against it. I imagine most people will have forgotten about it by the time this book is published.

If Milton were alive when that happened, I could clearly imagine him saying, "What a bunch of idiots. Nevertheless! Where were we?" He would have dismissed it, called it what it was, and moved on.

....

"Nevertheless!" is a magical exclamation because it puts you in the driver's seat of your response. You will always have the option to plunge into grief or frustration, and sometimes it's called for. But if it's not serving you, remember, it's not the only option. You can release. Let it go. "Nevertheless!" that shit.

Ask: Are we in Corsica?

Okay, not to make light of banishment, but Seneca has something to teach us about seeing the opportunity around us. In 41 AD, the emperor Claudius banished Seneca to the island of Corsica after an accusation of adultery with the emperor's niece.

I don't doubt Seneca's exile was horrible in many ways—not the least being that he was torn away from his family. But he was not in prison. I mean, have you *heard* of Corsica? Have you heard of it because you've been on a glorious vacation there or ogled the natural beauty of this Mediterranean island with breathtaking beaches? Do you want to google-image-search it *right now?*

I think of this story whenever I see a business or leaders feeling stuck in a corner, down on their luck, desperately grasping to get back to where they want to be. It's worth looking around a second to ask, "Wait, is it in fact gorgeous here? *Are we in Corsica?*"

- Maybe turnover is high, but is it an opportunity bring in fresh skillsets?
- Maybe a product or market didn't work out, but do we now have a bench of talent we can shift to innovative work we've never had capacity for until now?

- Maybe business is booming and people are exhausted, but can we finally pay out bonuses and declare a "business is great" company holiday?

Are there things to learn? New things to try? Time and space or money that wasn't available before? Should we maybe all get umbrella drinks while we're here?

Be the narrator of your team

Leadership is not cheerleading. I should know because I've done both. (I'll have to drum up an embarrassing high school picture somewhere. And if we ever meet in person, feel free to ask me to show you my cheerleading scars, complete with implanted plates and screws.)

Cheerleaders have one job: keep it positive! Because I've never known a cheer that went

It's okay! It's okay!
Though we've tried,
We suck today!

Leaders have quite another job (among many), and that's to help their people feel seen and supported so that they may tackle anything that comes their way.

It's common, though, for leaders to confuse the two jobs. Somehow it *feels* like you, as a leader, need to stay positive and encouraging, even if things are going off the rails and you're personally scared, exhausted, or both. I'd like to officially protest this vision of the ever-confident, show-no-fear leader. It's exhausting for the leader and simply not effective.

Perhaps at some point in your life you've been woken by someone saying, "Rise and shine, sleepyhead!" If you were half asleep and still exhausted, did that enthusiastic encouragement make you want to leap out of bed and start your day? I imagine it more likely made you want to throw your pillow at that person and go back to sleep. Perhaps you've even been that person yourself? (Duck!)

I was talking with a friend recently who was on an intense sprint with his team. He was working all hours and knew the team was, too. And yet he felt the need to present as positive and encouraging, because the leader above him was presenting this way. He said to me, privately, "This is insane! Can't we just say this is insane?"

Adam Grant says it well: "In hard times, urging people to stay positive doesn't boost their resilience. It denies their reality."

So what does it sound like to be a narrator for your team? How can you help your team process the moment, whether good or bad? How can you help them find both an outlet and perspective so you can carry on with hope?

It might sound like this:

All right team, this week has been intense, no? I did not expect to run into all those glitches, and I hated that we had to work late on Wednesday. I'm personally kind of annoyed and exhausted by it all, but also I feel hopeful that we're past it now and we'll definitely know for next time how to prepare. How are you all feeling?

This is only a 5- to 10-minute discussion or even a Slack post, but it can be enormously helpful for people to feel seen and validated.

Ugh, I keep saying I won't cite the business case for these things because feeling validated is nice in and of itself! But I hear my grad school professors "ahem"-ing in my head that there are lots of academics doing legit research on this and it's good to share.

Barsade and Gibson are two such academics who studied top management teams and found that "greater diversity in a team's trait positive affect was related to poorer corporate financial performance." Or in non-academic speak, when people in a team were all feeling different things, performance suffered.

Imagine a team where one person is having a grand ol' time, another is struggling, one is confused, and one doesn't fucking care. Doesn't feel like a very cozy team, does it? Are they tracking together? Empathizing with and supporting each other? Are they seeing the same things?

It doesn't have to be the case that everyone sees everything as great or everyone is down in the dumps. But everyone *should* be able to process those highs and lows—even if simultaneous—together.

Dr. Becky Kennedy shares the phrase "two things are true" to describe how you can validate the feelings of those around you, while not denying simple facts of the situation. That can sound like this:

- "We can be proud of what we accomplished this week *and* never want to repeat that intensity ever again."
- "We can love our client *and* admit they make us kind of crazy!"

Two things are true.

Honestly, it comes down to this. If a colleague or leader can confirm that you're not crazy and that it *is* an insane way to work, you can at least get on with the insanity knowing you're seen.

And finally, don't be afraid to narrate good moments as well!

"Team, is it just me, or did we fucking kill it in that meeting?!"

I can't tell you how many times a great meeting will end and everyone is silent after just waiting for the leader to declare that it was indeed great. No one wants to say, "That was awesome, team!" just for the leader to be like "Yeah, about that . . ." So if you're the leader: CALL THE WIN!

Don't burn until you're on fire.

MY HUSBAND, Brad Groff
What I woke up to every morning in
our last apartment

Conduct a pre-mortem

Have you ever been at a project kick-off chuckling to yourself because you know *exactly* how the project is going to go?

Like, there's no way we're completing all the upfront work in one week, so we're going to be behind our project plan by week two. Oh, and for sure our partner team is going to need more turnaround time. We're going to be working super late before that big meeting. And this bicoastal team is definitely going to get annoyed with each other's time boundaries.

You've seen this movie before, haven't you?

A pre-mortem is a moment to lay out that movie as we see it unfolding, and then change the script!

To do that, you're going to need some prospective hindsight. According to *Harvard Business Review*, "Prospective hindsight—imagining that an event has already occurred—increases the ability to correctly identify reasons for future outcomes by 30 percent."

The how-to:

Block off the time: You could do this exercise in as little as 30 minutes as part of a team kick-off, or use a full 90 minutes for a mission critical and/or complex initiative.

Define the bounds: What do you want to pre-mortem? Is it a specific project or initiative? A quarter? It's best if there's a discrete start and end to what you want to pre-mortem so people can envision the end point where you're declaring victory/failure.

Design the session: Pick a person to be your facilitator/Dungeons & Dragons Master and create your agenda.

Here's a sample agenda you could adapt for your team:

Welcome and check-in, because always.

Frame the session by explaining that the point of the exercise is not to be negative and blame-y, but to be superheroes that can see the future and bend it to your liking.

Put people in the future using "prospective hindsight." Instead of saying "What do you think could go wrong?" say, "Close your eyes and imagine it's the last day of our project. We're sitting around the project table with some cookies someone picked up to celebrate the end, but no one feels celebratory. As you look forlornly at your cookie, think about what went wrong over the past three months."

Ask people to identify the reasons for failure, individually and quietly, on sticky notes. Share the reasons for failure by asking one person to share their notes, and invite others to add their notes if they have similar ones. Continue until everyone's notes are up. Then, invite a time-boxed discussion of what they see: "What feels most probable?" "What would be most devastating if it happened?"

Ask people to generate ideas for prevention, individually and quietly. It could be something like, "Each week, let's do a bandwidth check, asking ourselves what parts of our work feel well staffed and which components need more love."

Ask people to read and congregate their notes.

Invite everyone to vote on the solutions they want to carry forward. Together, identify the top three to five ideas that you want to put into practice on your team, as well as any next steps (e.g., Marie will add a bandwidth check into our weekly meeting).

Debrief by asking things like, "In what ways do you feel more prepared?" "What ideas make you feel most sturdy?"

A pre-mortem is not meant to create paranoia and anxiety—just the opposite. Consider, for example, that you likely don't actively worry about spilling coffee. Why? Because your ability to clean a spill is more robust than the risk. You are confident that you can handle it.

The same can be true in business. The reason we hold anxiety and ruminate on possible unfortunate events is that we are *not* confident in our ability to handle them. A pre-mortem helps you build the team's capability so the team is more robust than the risks it will face. And that's not all! A pre-mortem helps you set better conditions up front so those risks are less likely to manifest in the first place.

I realize that last bit sounded like a 3 am pre-mortem infomercial. Unfortunately, a pre-mortem cannot cut through a shoe.

Note: When I first heard of a pre-mortem, I thought, "What a fucking downer!" You can certainly do a pre-vivo and instead ask what went right in the project, coming with ideas for making those things true.

Closing thought

There have been many times I've felt so wrapped up in a project that everything else in life felt like a distraction—the need to eat, sleep, and even talk to others who were not colleagues. My emotional state was completely dependent on the state of my work.

Work can be addicting in the way that you put on your VR headset and it becomes your entire reality. It's so easy to get sucked in, to lose perspective. Sometimes, the best way to keep it cool is to *care a little less*—not because your work is unimportant or small, but because the world is so very big! Work is simply not everything. There is *more*.

There are lilac bushes.
Jazz trios.
Childhood friends who don't care what your résumé says.
Black-and-white pictures of your grandparents looking ravishing.
The smell of old books.
Kites.

It's a big, beautiful world out there, and I don't want either of us to miss it.

. . . ONE OF MANY IN OUR LIVES

6

YOU ARE THE DEFENDER OF DATE NIGHTS, CROSSWORD PUZZLES, AND YOUR HEALTH

I've spent a whole lot of pages talking about how to make work joyful (or at least less stressful). Now it's time to switch gears and acknowledge that work is only one joy of many available to us in life.

The trouble with work is that it can be greedy. Sometimes you may work too much because that's what the job requires. Other times it might be because you find it fun and even addicting. But either way, there's a cost, and it can't be avoided.

When you overwork, you underlive.

Our time is finite, and if more is spent working, less is spent on date nights, crossword puzzles, your health, or many other parts of your life that are important to you. Under no circumstances should you take your laptop on your date night in a quest to "have it all."

So what are we risking if we overwork? If we don't defend our time?

Sometimes it helps to do the math. My goal is to fill you with existential dread for a hot second, so hold on. I'm not sure what life circumstance best describes you, so here's a buffet of terror-inducing thoughts to choose from:

- If you have an eight-year-old kid, that means you probably have 10 more years of them living with you. But by the time they're 13 they'll be much more interested in spending time with their friends than with you. So let's call it five more years of cozy kid time as you know it. Five precious years. Out of your hopefully 90+ years on the planet. Or put differently, by the time they turn 18, 90 percent of your parent-child time together is likely already spent. After that, it'll probably be a couple of visits a year.

- If you have living parents, you're looking at the previous example but from the other side. Let's say your parents are 70 years old. If they have 20 more years, that's a pretty good run. Maybe they live in a different city than you, though, and you only see each other twice a year at holidays. Are you okay with only seeing your parents 40 more times *ever*? Know too (and I know this well) that not all of those years are created equal. Right now is likely the healthiest your parents will ever be.

- If you're 60 years old, you'll hopefully have 30+ more years, but like your parents, not all of them will be equally healthy. Your risk of cardiovascular disease, neurodegenerative disease, cancer, and a host of other tragedies increases dramatically with age. If you want to be conservative, you're looking at 20 more good birthday parties.

None of it is fun to think about, but the alternative is worse. In the words of Seneca, "How many have laid waste to your life when you weren't aware of what you were losing, how much was wasted ... how little of your own life was left to you."

When you miss life, no one tells you you're missing it. Except, I suppose, that's exactly what I'm trying to do here, just in case you are.

P.S. If you're 25, I hope you're enjoying your metabolism. In all seriousness, you've got a great head start in thoughtfully considering what "the good life" looks like to you.

IN THIS CHAPTER

TIME IS THE NEW MONEY

Work is addicting
....

Delayed gratification is overrated
....

The perils of above and beyond
....

Purpose is alluring
....

Your bones will tell you
where to be
....

Excel doesn't care
if you live or die
....

Dread by the numbers
....

Bob has seen enough
....

Not busy is possible
....

HOW TO DETOX
FROM OVERWORK

Understand the
psychology of overwork
....

Ask yourself: Do I want that prize?
....

Know who gets the best of you
....

Make people whole
....

Detox your belief system
....

Detox your behaviors
....

TIME IS THE NEW MONEY

Work is addicting

I'd like to introduce you to Excel, Goddess of Workaholism. She tries to hang with the Muse and even dresses up like her to try to trick you, but make no mistake, she's the evil one. She has all sorts of clever stories she tells us to keep us addicted and grinding. Some of these stories even make complete sense. Nonetheless, they conspire to keep us from the most beautiful parts of our lives. Excel whispers in your ear:

- "Once you get off the treadmill, it's very hard to get back on."
- "You're in your peak wealth-building years—this is the time to double down."
- "You're not going to earn that 'exceeds expectations' performance review working 40 hours a week."
- "Your kids don't understand that you're working late for their future."
- "Your partner doesn't understand how important your work is."
- "Your clients, customers, colleagues—they need you. You have to show up for them."
- "Your work is changing the world. You have to keep pushing."
- "If you take your foot off the gas, your colleagues will get promoted over you."
- "It will be worth it when you get the raise."
- "It will be worth it when you retire comfortably."
- "You can sleep when you're dead."

She is oh so convincing and knows just what argument will hook you. She's alluring and addicting, like some kind of corporate siren, and will take the best parts of your life if you let her.

Excel works only in one direction. She'll take and take and take some more. She'll make you think it's normal to be working every night; will make you think all the cool kids are doing it; will make you feel like you have to run just to keep up. While you are mortal, Excel is not. She will draw you into her bottomless pit and make you feel that it's SO VERY IMPORTANT that you stay in that pit. And here's the sneakiest part: she makes you *want* to be there.

When employees want boundaries around work and organizations are trying to make them do too much of it, it's not easy, but a pretty decent solution is union contracts.

But I suspect you may fall in the same Stockholm Syndrome-y camp I do where we don't work so much because it feels bad and we think we need to. *We work so much because it feels good.* We work for a sense of accomplishment, because it feels good to deliver for someone or to strut our intellectual stuff. We work hard to catch up, to get ahead, to be seen as going above and beyond. None of this is inherently bad, mind you! That's what makes Excel so tricky. The badness all lives in the opportunity cost.

Delayed gratification is overrated

I've thought a lot about the virtues of work ethic and delayed gratification. Perhaps you remember the famous marshmallow experiment, where a researcher put kids alone in a room and set a single marshmallow in front of them. He said, "I'll be back in fifteen minutes. If you haven't eaten the marshmallow, I'll give you an extra one when I get back."

This study was done in 1972, and the children were followed for decades after. What was the difference between the kids who could delay their gratification and the kids who were like, "GET IN MY MOUTH"?

The kids who delayed gratification ended up having higher SAT scores, lower levels of substance abuse, lower levels of obesity, better responses to stress, better social skills, and generally better scores in a range of other life measures. It makes total sense, doesn't it? They became the adults who could study now and play later, work out now for a healthy body later, save now to build wealth later, and so on.

I've always been the same. Tell me to endure something and I'll endure it. I've rarely doubted this ability is a good thing. But have we taken it too far?

It's one thing to delay the gratification of some hedonistic, bad-for-you pleasure like a box of cookies. It's quite another to delay the gratification of things like time with those we love and enjoying the beauty of the world around us.

In the words of Thich Nhat Hanh, "We are very good at preparing to live, but not very good at living. We know how to sacrifice ten years for a diploma, and we are willing to work very hard to get a job, a car, a house, and so on. But we have difficulty remembering that we are alive in the present moment, the only moment there is for us to be alive." The feeling of never-enoughness can sometimes make us feel like the present moment isn't even ours; it's the input to the success of future-us. But what if we already have—and are—enough? The parable of the fisherman and the businessman (aka Excel in a suit) comes to mind.

One day a fisherman was lying on a beautiful beach, fishing pole propped up in the sand with his single line cast into the sparkling blue sea. He was enjoying the warmth of the sun on his skin, the gentle breeze, and the prospect of catching a fish.

As he reveled in the moment, a businessman came walking down the beach, trying to shake off the stress of his day. He noticed the fisherman with his single line cast and wondered why he wasn't working harder for himself and his family. It was noon on a Tuesday, after all.

Now he didn't want to be a jerk, but he felt compelled to say *something*. Maybe the fisherman didn't know how much upside he had! He decided to walk over.

"You know, if you prop up three lines and start working with a net, you could catch so many more fish!"

The fisherman replied, "I suppose so... If I did, what would that get me?"

"Well, you'd catch and sell a lot more fish and use the money to buy bigger nets!"

"Hmm... and then what would *that* get me?"

"You could buy a bigger boat, of course! And hire some people to work for you!" The businessman was beginning to think the fisherman was missing the entire point.

"Let's say I had the boat and the employees. What would *that* get me?"

"Don't you understand?! You could build up a whole fleet of boats, scale your enterprise, and become so rich you'll never have to work again! You can spend the rest of your days sitting on this beach, enjoying the sun and the breeze!"

The fisherman smiled.

"And what do you think I'm doing right now?"

The perils of above and beyond

When I was a teacher, my goal was for every one of my students to get an A. I felt that if an A meant "You learned everything you were supposed to learn!" and "You can do all the skills we practiced!" then why wouldn't it be my goal—if not the definition of my job—to help all students get there?

Of course, education (and business) loves a good forced ranking. Many of my colleagues argued that we need to define B as "good" so that the students who want/need extra challenge can go above and beyond to get the A. As so often is the case, the norms of school bleed into the norms of organizations, and all companies want those A-student employees who go above and beyond. Or in performance review parlance, who "exceed expectations."

We shouldn't just work less because it makes us better workers. We should work less because it makes us better people.

SIMONE STOLZOFF

This has always given me pause. It's one thing to expect that of students who are learning for their own benefit. It's quite another to expect that of employees who are working for the benefit of their organizations.

Did you know that one of the most common academic definitions of employee engagement is whether employees are devoting "discretionary effort"? On the surface it makes sense. You see an employee going above and beyond the role, devoting time and energy outside of work hours— discretionary time—and you say to yourself, "That employee is engaged! They're SO into it. Gotta get more of those folks."

It's no wonder why organizations want the Above-and-Beyonders—it's free labor! But we shouldn't kid ourselves where that discretionary effort comes from. It comes from the bedtime stories that employee is not reading to their children. From the exercise class that employee never went to. From the sleep that employee never got. It comes from somewhere; we just don't like to think about the cost.

And the truth is the leader won't see it. We don't see the frustrated spouse or the blood pressure report or the lonely kid or the anti-anxiety medications. Employees are taught to shield these things as the ultimate NSFW content.

So it's easy to see why a leader in this position might say, "They wanted to! I didn't make them," and that may be true. It's possible they *really were* that into their work, that they took pride in it, that it was meaningful to them—and you know those aren't bad things. The trouble comes when, as an organizational baseline, employees are seen only as meeting expectations when they're *exceeding* expectations. Or more simply, when overwork is *expected.*

The thing is, that wasn't the deal. We have employment contracts for a reason. I'll give you this time/effort/skill and you give me this money. How funny would it be if we expected employers to exceed expectations with their paychecks? Ugh . . . just the usual two weeks' pay. I expected more! My company is just not going above and beyond like I hoped.

Now that I've exhaled that rant, let me say, as you know, I also believe in doing great work. Impactful, captivating, generous, needle-moving work. I just believe that that work should be accounted for in your day job. It's the employer's responsibility to realistically consider what it takes for an employee, a team, a function, or an organization to do that kind of powerful work, and then set up employment contracts, objectives, key results, and deadlines that allow for that work within the confines of the workday. In other words, without breaking their promises.

Otherwise, your business runs on extracting more than your fair share from employees. It runs on breaching your employment agreements. It runs on baiting and switching employees, often with a story about how purposeful their work is, ignoring that their time spent on family, friends, health, leisure, and rest is also purposeful. The solution is hard but simple: hire more people or reduce the work.

Huh, look at that... I guess my rant was not over.

Okay, I'm taking a deep breath, and now I need to say that this riles me up *because* I've been an Above-and-Beyonder all my life and often still am. My rant is hard to reconcile with my desire to go the extra mile for a client, even when that means putting on my figurative running shoes at 10 pm when I finally have time to focus.

From a leadership perspective, I take it as a personal failure when my project teams run hot. I scoped the work. There's no one but me to blame. For every project I scope, I try to bake in time for us to uphold the incredibly high standards we have for ourselves and our work and our clients. But it doesn't always work out that way. Although it may sound like I'm targeting leaders unfairly, I really do get how hard it is to do this because I've been a CEO. Hire more people? With what money? Reduce the work? How will we keep our business afloat? Oh, just raise prices. Ha!

But, ultimately, I believe that's why leaders are paid the big bucks: to figure this out.

Purpose is alluring

Let's talk about purpose: the biggest mind fuck of them all.

If Excel sees you starting to pull back from work, she reaches right up her sleeve for this ace.

If you've been overworking for years, if you've sacrificed bedtime stories and soccer games and your blood pressure and your relationship with your partner and countless nights of sleep and your mental health and calling your family, not to mention any kind of hobbies, letting something take higher priority than *your body* and *your family* . . . well, then your brain will be very incentivized to believe that that something was worth it. Because if it wasn't worth it, *then what the hell were you thinking*?

Cognitive dissonance describes the discomfort a person feels when their behavior does not align with their beliefs: for example, when a person has to hold both "my family and my health are the most important things to me" and "instead of spending time with my family or exercising, I chose to work late every night this week." Our brains detest cognitive dissonance and will do whatever they can to repair the contradiction.

And this is when Excel comes waltzing in with purpose on a platter.

- "Just think of the scale your company operates at. You're part of that."
- "You're not just writing marketing copy; you're changing the world through storytelling."
- "You're not mopping the floor. You're putting a man on the moon!"

Yes, we think as our brains start to relax, "That's right. That's why it's worth it. My work is that important. I'm setting an example for my children about what hard work is. Nothing worth doing was ever easy."

And while you are busy thinking that, your children go to bed wondering what was more important than them. Your partner goes to sleep without you. And your arteries start to stiffen, unaware of how very important you are.

Your bones will tell you where to be

Okay, now I feel like I've gotten in a fight with purpose and need to make up.

Let me be clear: Company purposes, personal purposes, these are good things. Especially for a company, having a stated purpose is about 10,000 times better than your default purpose being to make money.

Purpose is a tool, and just like any tool, it can be used for good or for evil. Unfortunately, it can be hard to tell if purpose is helping you find meaning, or if it's stabbing you in your sleep. The truth is I don't have a good litmus test to help you tell good purpose from stabby purpose. I, myself, just listen to my bones.

In the nine months I spent caring for my mom, I didn't give two shits about my professional purpose. When I was next to her, watching Rachael Ray in the hospital, sharing her cup of sorbet, I had not a doubt in the world that that's exactly where I was supposed to be. I knew it in my bones.

When I'm snuggled next to Arden at night and she's telling me all about the drama leading up to the talent show, I know in my bones that this is the nectar of life. Now, my bones don't always lean family. I'm not suggesting you spend your days just staring at the people you love. Like right now, I'm still in upstate New York on my little writer's getaway, decidedly away from my family and all caregiving. I've been writing all day every day with a profound sense of purpose and momentum. And someone just brought me a glass of prosecco, which really convinces my bones they're in the right place.

More often than not, though, I don't need to convince myself to work more. It's easy to work more. What's hard is convincing myself I'm the defender of the beautiful parts of my life outside of work.

I have a vivid memory of staying at my grandpa's house about eight years ago. I was there with my mom visiting him. He must have been 93 at the time and was as strong and loving and joyful as ever. He and my mom were downstairs after dinner enjoying each other's company. I had taken a few days off work for this visit, but there was this one proposal I wanted to get done, and so I left them to work upstairs for the remainder of the night.

Did we win the work? No.

Does the person I sent the proposal to remember they got it on Friday instead of Monday? No.

Does the person I sent the proposal to remember the proposal at all? Still no.

Do they remember me? Maybe, at best.

Would I give my right arm to have another shot at that evening—to sit in the warmth of my grandfather's home, chatting about this and that with my mom and grandpa into the night? *In a heartbeat.*

The next time you find yourself telling someone you love, "Ten more minutes," just shut the computer and go to them. Trust me.

Excel doesn't care if you live or die

If your inner Excel isn't backing down yet, let's try this fun fact:

For around 50 percent of people who experience cardiovascular disease (e.g., heart attack, stroke), can you guess the first symptom they experience?

Chest pain, you say?

Shortness of breath?

Surprisingly, incorrect. The first symptom is . . . drumroll, please . . .

SUDDEN DEATH.

Is that the kind of roulette you should be playing? Because I bet you *can* guess the biggest contributors to the development of ASCVD ("athero-sclerotic cardiovascular disease" is hard to say quickly). Beyond genetics, it's poor diet, physical inactivity, lack of sleep, psychological stress, and smoking/other substance abuse.

"Sorry I'm late to the meeting—had to shove something in my mouth because I didn't have time to get out for lunch. I'm a bit off today because I was up late last night working. This upcoming meeting is stressing me out. I need a drink!"

I have one thing to say about this way of working: IT'S NOT WORTH IT.

And when I start to feel like it is, I know that's Excel talking. Trying to convince me of how important I am, how important this thing is, that it's worth my health.

Resist!

Dread by the numbers

I'll admit I may be laying it on a little thick with all the sad children and dead relatives and the prospect of your own sudden death. Let's take a break from my heartstring marionette act and look to the data:

According to the American Institute of Stress,

- 83 percent of US workers suffer from work-related stress;
- about one million Americans miss work each day because of stress;
- 76 percent of US workers report that workplace stress affects their personal relationships; and
- depression-induced absenteeism costs US businesses $51 billion a year, as well as an additional $26 billion in treatment costs.

Care for another? According to Headspace's workforce attitudes toward mental health report,

- 89 percent of employees surveyed say they've felt moderate to extreme stress over the past month, with 49 percent saying they feel a sense of dread at least once per week;
- respondents point to instability and unpredictability at work, overwhelming expectations to take on more job responsibilities, and higher expectations and fear of not meeting them as the top three drivers of their dread.

DREAD. That's a big word, don't you think? It tells me we've gotten something massively wrong.

Bob has seen enough

Bob is back for another mission. He's reported back on the almighty Google Calendar, and his fellow aliens were fascinated to know more. He decides to find out how the Google Calendar organizes her kingdom.

The first thing he observes is the prevalent 5/2 split of things called weekdays and the weekend. "Huh," Bob thinks to himself, "seems like a lot of work. Not the split I would have designed."

He reads on the internet: In 1926, Henry Ford standardized a five-day workweek, instead of the prevalent six days, without reducing employees' pay.

"Wait, the 5/2 split is an *improvement*? Well, it must be sustainable if it's so prevalent…"

Then he reads in some report that 89 percent of employees surveyed say they've felt moderate to extreme stress over the past month, with 49 percent saying they feel a sense of dread at least once per week.

"This Google Calendar overlord must be evil! Five days of constant stress-inducing work?"

Then he reads:

1 On your computer, open Google Calendar.
2 Click the space next to the date you want to add an event to.
3 Add a title and time for your event.
4 Click Save. Calendar will automatically create an event at the time you set.

"THE HUMANS ARE DOING THIS TO THEMSELVES? I'm going home."

Not busy is possible

Sue: Milton never seemed busy. There was never this feeling of busy-ness or tight scheduling that I think a lot of people feel now, going from this to that and, oh, I don't have time for that other thing. I don't think we ever experienced time in the way most people experience it today, where you feel like there's never enough to do what you need to do.

Milton would come in to work and say, "Shirley [his wife] made this amazing pasta alle vongole with clams, and she did this with the butter, and we got this beautiful pot..." And whatever we were doing would just wait, because we were talking about spaghetti and clams, and he wanted to share dinner stories.

HOW TO DETOX
FROM OVERWORK

Understand the psychology of overwork

First, it might be helpful for us to identify the drug(s) we are detoxing from. I won't even pretend that this is a MECE (mutually exclusive, collectively exhaustive) list. It completely ignores overwork that comes from things like the math, strategy, and power problems I talked about in chapter 4.

Instead, we're going to dive headfirst into the most sinister of them all: the psychology problem. There are aspects of our psychology that, when balanced, keep us interested in work. But like video games and drugs, work can also hijack the reward centers in our brain and keep us hooked on behaviors that feel good in the moment but ultimately don't serve us. So what, exactly, is work addicting us to?

Accomplishment: Accomplishment is a wonderful thing that *should* produce a sense of pleasure. But accomplishment as a drug means that with each success comes the feeling of never-enoughness.

Validation: For those of us who particularly love to bask in the glow of positive feedback, it can feel like we need to keep producing new and novel output to feed the stream of praise. No one leverages this better than social media companies.

Status: In centuries past, status was conferred by birth, title, class. Now it's conferred by professional role. In other words, executive vice president is the new duchess. Don't get me wrong, neither are awesome systems, but it's important to consider how they impact our motivation. Consider the leisure class in the days of yore. They didn't need a professional title because they held familial titles, so they were free to enjoy their garden parties. Now we work for our titles. It's an improvement to be sure, since it at least appears to reflect meritocracy (though I'm aware that's a generous description; privilege is no joke). But what it means functionally is that incessant work is a sign of high status, which in turn means safety and power—what status has always meant. It's no wonder the first question we ask at cocktail parties is, "What do you do?" Perhaps we're genuinely interested, but the question is also a proxy for "How fancy are you?"

Identity: When people (typically mothers) step away from work to become full-time caregivers, one of the most jarring parts is losing a sense of self, as in, "Who even am I without my profession to identify me?" In the same way, it is so common and understandable that caregivers, retirees, sabbatical-takers, and the like, when asked, "What do you do?" can be heard saying, "I used to be a..."

Safety: We all need a living wage. But far too often we inflate what it is we need to live. Nobody needs the expensive house, cars, private school, and overpriced socks. But we tend to lock ourselves into these lifestyles and then convince ourselves that overwork is the only way to sustain them.

Power: The shadow side of getting excited to put your stamp on the world through brilliant work is that sometimes you wind up like Arden. At the age of four, with her brand-new stamp in hand, she set about trying to stamp everything from our carpet to my forehead. Power is great when you can wield it, but watch out because it'll wield you right back. Like every item in this list, the dose makes the poison.

Ask yourself: Do I want that prize?

Sometimes I think about Finland's former 35-year-old prime minister.

Most days I feel like I'm killing it because I'm doing good work at work, I'm taking great care of my health, I'm supporting my dad and my daughter, and I'm writing this book! But some days I feel like I could be doing so much more. For example, I have not been the leader of a nation for five years now.

If I google "get into politics" tomorrow, how long before I can feasibly run for president?

I know, I'm being dramatic. I should at least run for Senate first.

I recognize that I'm spiraling when these thoughts rush in. Becoming president is an extreme example, but it only takes a good social media scrolling sesh for my ambition monster to rear its green head. In these moments, I'm awash in both questioning and mourning the classically ambitious parts of myself that have ebbed in recent years:

- Is it bad that I'm not pushing my way up as hard as I can?
- Is it bad that I'm not exhausting myself?*
- Am I a bad feminist for not doing so?

*If I haven't "exhausted" myself, by definition, I had more to give to my career but chose not to.

In these moments, I try to regulate by channeling my inner fisherman. I ask myself, "If I went after this success I'm envying and it works out, what would that get me? Do I want that prize?" Or DIWTP, if you want to put it on a bracelet.

As I am the boss of my life, I try to remember that my job is not to follow ambition for its own sake. It's to ensure that if I'm working really hard at something, I actually want the prize at the end. It's like spending $50 to conquer balloon darts at the carnival and winning! Only to be rewarded with having to carry around a five-foot teddy bear the rest of the day.

Do I want to be president? I didn't even like running for VP of student council in fifth grade. So no, I do not want that prize.

I do not want that prize.

I do not want that prize.

I do not want that prize.

It takes a few times before my brain considers believing it.

If you're working hard at something—scaling a business, interviewing for a new role, starting a project, gunning for a promotion—I invite you to ask yourself, "If I succeed, what would that get me? And do I want that prize?"

Only you know the answer! I hope it's a ravishing "yes." And if it's not, well, that's the first step in moving along to the next carnival game.

Know who gets the best of you

"You're not doing your best!"

Arden yelled that at me one night when she was four years old after she caught me turning two pages of her bedtime story at a time so I could get back to work faster.

At the time I felt immediately defensive. I thought, "Well of course I'm not doing my best! My best—my creativity and energy and extra miles—that's reserved for work, and let me tell you, work takes its FULL SHARE before anyone else can call dibs." At home, I was doing the minimum. Chores would pile up, and Arden would whittle away time in front of a screen. I mean, I would say I was "doing my best," but the truth is I was doing my best with the energy I had left over. Arden was getting work's scraps.

I did not like that. Full stop.

Today everyone takes turns, and it's good. Some days work gets the freshest, smartest parts of me. But more days it's Arden. My dad gets some. Brad gets some. My friends get some. And I, of course, do too (the house always wins). It's how I keep work a source of joy—one of many in my life.

Make people whole

We've talked about detoxing from the drug of work, but what happens when you're the drug dealer? What do you do when you really need the freshest, smartest parts of your team? The truth is, sometimes my teams do work late. Sometimes we find ourselves with more work than we have hours and people. And sometimes it's still important to nail the work and make it brilliant.

This is how I handle these moments.

The PM and I scan the horizon for crunch times, and we alert the team in advance: This can sound like, "The client meeting on Friday is coming up fast. To be safe, we might want to plan on late nights Wednesday and Thursday for final prep. If you can be there, this is the official nudge to go about alerting any significant others. If you can't be there, it's okay, truly. Between all of us we'll make it work. We'll try to make it fun and order dinner and play some tunes."

We make it infrequent: Sometimes something unexpectedly needs to be redone, there's a dependency we didn't realize, or something just takes longer than the project plan accounted for. It's a deviation from the plan. It is *not* the normal course of business. I bank that learning so I can do a better job scoping the work next time.

I have already made the deposits: In these moments, as a leader, I hope my team will show up for me and the client and the work. As we talked about in chapter 3, this is taking a withdrawal. I hope I've invested in the team's naps and rest before getting to this point, but if not, I make sure I can pay back that time post-crunch. If time equals money in business, and I would never borrow money from someone without paying them back, why would I think any differently about time?

And when the crunch is over, you know what I do? I share all of my grati-tude with the team, and I fuck off. Sleep! Family! Queso! Exercise! Reality TV! Or whatever my little overworking heart desires.

Detox your belief system

Maybe you're thinking, "I don't particularly want the prizes I'm getting, but what do I do? Like seriously, I can't quit my job."

The truth is I don't know what will work for you, because if we're talking solutions, they could range from quitting your corporate job to become a solopreneur to taking three deep breaths every morning. Even reading this, you might think the first is impossible and the second is stupid.

The challenge is that overwork is an everything problem: a government policy problem, a societal cultural problem, an economic problem, an identity problem, and 27 other problems. I'm not an expert in public policy or economics, but I do know a lot about what individuals and leaders can do to make work life a little better despite the larger systems. To avoid boiling the ocean (don't worry, Bob, I don't mean it), my goal is to equip you with at least one thing that will help you defeat Excel.

Consider these my best swordplay techniques. If you're most interested in deprogramming from a dominant culture of overwork, start with this beliefs exercise. If instead you're thinking, "Just tell me what to do and I will fake it till I make it," then start with behaviors in the next section.

Let's dive into some fundamental, existential questions about your relationship with yourself, your life, and your work:

1 When I overwork, who else is paying the price?
2 Am I less important at work than I think I am?
3 What moments do I want more of in my life?
4 Can I accept the trade-offs of not overworking?
5 Can I start to glamorize balance?

1. When I overwork, who else is paying the price?

It's one thing for you to willingly overwork and pay the price yourself. It's quite another to take the payment for it out of someone else's bank account. When I overwork, I ask myself, "Where is that withdrawal coming from?" For me, it's the time I would be spending with Brad, Arden, and my dad.

Soon after Arden was born, I became extremely careful about crossing the street. I used to jaywalk like a proper New Yorker ("I'm walkin' here!"), but then a thought struck me: if I were to get run over by a car, not only would it be true that "I got run over" but that "Arden's mom got run over," and somehow that made all the difference. I had to protect Arden's mom!

Similarly, when I overwork, I not only think, "I work late a lot," but I also think, "Arden's mom works late a lot." And is that what I want for her?

I chose the word "defender" in this chapter specifically because if you have any dependents or those you care for or even friendships you value, it's likely they can't defend themselves against your overwork. Arden can't tell the client no. My dad can't decline the meeting invite. That's all up to me. Am I going to be good at defending them? Will I be a high performer for them?

This is a shitty question to answer, and I don't blame you if you don't want to. But it's here just in case: Who pays when you overwork? What price do they pay?

If it matters, make time for it.

IAN SANDERS

2. Am I less important at work than I think?

I write this one with love. You are 1,000 percent important to all the friends, family, partners, and pets who love you. But at work? Remember: even leaders of nations are replaceable.

Sometimes it takes a pressure cooker to reveal that truth. The day I learned of my mom's terminal cancer diagnosis was hands down the worst day of my life to date. I remember lying in my bed, staring out the window, saying over and over to Brad, "I'm not processing this. I don't know how to process this. I'm not processing this." But something in me knew what I needed to do. I needed to get to my mom. I booked a flight to Chicago. And I needed to get everything else out of the way.

I messaged my colleagues that I was out, starting now, for the foreseeable future. I wrote down everything that was on my plate with instructions for taking over each thing, and I pressed send. I didn't even ask permission for leave because I was not going to take no for an answer. I knew I was in an incredibly caring organization and I was not going to lose my job over it, but even if I had thought it was a risk, I would have done just the same. This is what savings are for. What future earnings are for. What this time was for was being with my mom. And most of all, I *wanted* to be with her. It would be six months and a combination of sick days, partially paid family leave, and unpaid leave before I returned to consulting. I don't regret a single minute.

At the time it honestly felt like an easy decision. Meteors flying into your life have a way of making things really clear. I'm not suggesting that if you have healthy parents you quit your job to go stare at them all day. But it's worth keeping in mind this truth: *You are more important than you think to those who love you. You are less important than you think to those who employ you.*

Imagine you quit your job tomorrow. Who would take on your work? What would the company do?

3. What moments do I want more of in my life?

When I'm in Excel's grip, usually the only thing I'm trying to get more of is reality TV and takeout in bed. It's my salve: the brain-dulling entertainment, belly-pleasing calories, and deep pleasure of eschewing all formality, including tables and chairs. Maybe for you it's playing video games or scrolling or some other dopamine-friendly activity.

But sometimes when I am deep in these moments, I do wonder, Is this peak life for me? Is this what I'm working so hard for? Is it okay that calling my family feels like a chore, stopping to cook dinner feels like a distraction, and exercising feels like some kind of masochism I don't have time for?

If this resonates, let me be clear: I hold no judgment. Just last night Brad and I were both reading before bed instead of scrolling on our phones (we're trying to improve our sleep hygiene), and I thought to myself, Wait, is this what some people do all the time? Is this normal and we've just been missing it? I've had the exact same thought about cooking dinner: Wait, this is actually fun! HAS COOKING DINNER WITH JAZZ MUSIC ON AND A GLASS OF PORT BEEN HERE AND AVAILABLE TO ME THIS WHOLE TIME? I don't know, it just felt like something retirees did.

I've gotten better about maximizing the moments that matter. Arden and I have a routine where we read together in her bed. She reads Wings of Fire and I read Agatha Christie. I'm embarrassed to admit there have been times when I thought of her bedtime routine as a detour that was keeping me from getting back to work. I have been there, and now I am here: totally and completely in love with that time.

I want to hear about your happy place! If you could freeze time and live forever in one moment, what would it be? Draw or sketch.

4. Can I accept the trade-offs of not overworking?

I'm not going to pretend that overwork is not productive. As you know, I 100 percent believe rest is necessary for brilliant work, but sometimes "the math problem" is real. There's just a lot of work, and if you can do more of it, brilliantly or not, promotions follow.

Harvard economist Claudia Goldin's quote on this topic blew my mind: "Women don't step back from work because they have rich husbands. They have rich husbands because they step back from work." In other words, if you have the capacity to work all the time while everything else in your life is tended to, well that's pretty attractive from an employer perspective, whether they say so out loud or not.

Truthfully, I don't know what to do about this at a societal level. I know I went through a lot of "How did I end up here?" feelings when I was working part-time and Brad was working full-time. Am I a bad feminist? How did I end up the caregiver? This could certainly be a whole other book, but here's what I know:

Time with family and those we love *really* matters—for everyone. If you don't bank that time, you will die without it. Time doesn't tap you on the shoulder as it's passing you by. What kind of prize is it to be successful but working constantly? Is that the goal? It's not my goal. Looks like a five-foot teddy bear to me.

I always used to think of myself as a goat in any new role. Not *the* GOAT, but *a* goat. You know how goats are always trying to climb to the highest peak around them, whether that's a mountain or the top of a car? That was me, trying to figure out how to get to the top of any organization. Maybe it was 16 years of rankings-based school, but it seemed like that was the whole point. Now, I've decided:

I don't want to.
I don't choose that.
I could!
But I don't.
I accept the trade-offs.

To be honest, I'm much more cat than goat now—always looking to make myself and my team a cozy bed in a corner of organizational sunlight.

Tell me the trade-offs—what you're confidently giving up. Get 'em out. Tell them, "I don't need you."

5. Can I start to glamorize balance?

Recently Brad and I were at Arden's swim meet talking to parents from another team. Their kids were in extra math classes, musical theater, and soccer—and we were already at a competitive swim meet for nine-year-olds who practice four times a week.

I started to spiral. Should Arden be doing more? What am I not thinking of? Am I closing doors for her? Honestly, I felt shitty and dysregulated about it. And then I wondered, Who would protect Arden's ability to daydream and find pleasure in a lazy afternoon if not us?

For clarity, I hold no judgment for the parents and kids who are doing it all. Some of those kids really dig those activities! Similarly, some people, at some points in their lives, love working all hours. But it sure as hell isn't all of us, all the time.

Tim Ferriss's book *The 4-Hour Workweek* did an excellent job of selling the dream of balance and freedom. As he says, "Perhaps I'm just getting old, but my definition of luxury has changed over time. Now, it's not about owning a lot of stuff. Luxury, to me, is feeling unrushed."

Swoon, right?! But unfortunately, that mindset has not permeated most organizations. In most companies, unrushed equals inefficient. So what can we do to model balance? To make it glamorous?

Leave loud and proud!

If you haven't heard of Summer Fridays, it's a corporate policy that permits employees to take off early (usually between noon and 2 pm) every Friday between Memorial Day and Labor Day. One leader I worked with would always make it a point to yell, "See you Monday!" as she headed out to anyone left in the office. A sentiment started to grow across her team that if you couldn't get yourself out the door to take advantage of Summer Fridays, that didn't make you a committed employee going above and beyond, it made you a failure at getting your work done efficiently.

Now I'm not trying to say we should be side-eye shaming each other. But if there's going to be any glamor at all on this issue, I'd sure prefer that the glamor sits on the side of balance. And because glamor is often sourced from power, it really matters what leaders do here.

What can you and your team do to flaunt the glamor of...

doing less, better work?

being so good at your work it takes you less time than other teams?

being such a project-planning sniper that you have time for a Do Nothing Day AND a nap?

P.S. If you post pictures of all your naps on a central Slack channel, you may ruffle some feathers. But posting a DND picture or two will, hopefully, show others that it's possible.

Detox your behaviors

The trouble with being a chronic overworker is that you've likely become very good at it. Not overworking can feel highly uncomfortable if you've been conditioned to always work before you play, to always serve others before yourself. These are sometimes good strategies, but when it comes to work, these strategies will suck you dry. As a client once shared with me, "I tell my team: the sooner you realize work is a bottomless pit, the happier you'll be."

So how do we stop furiously digging to the bottom of our never-ending work pits? I invite you to pick at least one of these three "when-then" statements to commit to for the next week:

Ask, "Do I want that prize?"

When I feel the urge to strive for, accept, or envy an opportunity...

Then I will stop and ask, "What would that get me? Do I want that prize?"

For clarity, the question is, Do *I* want that prize?

The question is NOT, Does society want me to want that prize? Does my family want me to want that prize? Has my education groomed me to want that prize? Do I feel "someone like me" should want that prize?

All those questions depend on something other than what you want. *You* need to want that prize. Because society is not carrying that five-foot teddy bear for you.

Think before committing

There are points in every project, quarter, or planning cycle when someone meters out work and you commit to executing. Your goal is to send up a big-ass flare whenever you spot these Commit Moments. For example, when someone messages you, "Hey, can you share that deck by end of week?" your brain should scream "COMMIT MOMENT."

When I recognize a Commit Moment...

Then I will stop and say, "Let me get back to you before I can commit."

Remember, there's always more than simply "yes" or "no" at your disposal. As much as "no is a complete sentence," it can be really hard to sell that to a boss. If you need to, consider these alternatives:

- Yes, I can have it to you by end of next week, just not this week.
- Yes, I can take that on if I can take *x* off my plate or push it to next month.
- Yes, I can do that if Joy is available to work on it with me.
- Yes, I can deliver a draft this week, just not a final version.

After all, the goal is not to throw up hard boundaries at all costs. It's to do brilliant work that supports the business, *while* defending your time.

Prioritize life first

The default is often to let work ravage our lives, and then piece together the remaining scraps of time and dole them out to sleep, partners, exercise, hobbies, and the like. The trick is in remembering no one is going to *give* us time to do those things. We have to *take* it. So take it first:

When I plan my next week/month . . .

Then I will schedule workouts, dates (with partners, friends, kids, family), and doctor's appointments first—before work can claim that territory.

It is so much easier to decline a meeting due to a pre-existing appointment than it is to try to claw back time after it's been occupied by work. Get there first!

Closing thought

Sometimes we need a reminder of what it is we actually want—not what Excel or society tells us we should want. Tear out this page and cut out the statement. Carry it with you, pin it on a wall, or put it in the pocket of your stretchy pants.

Note: If your inner librarian just fainted from the thought of tearing a page from a book, you can certainly rewrite the phrase on another piece of paper. Or, you know, buy a second pristine copy. That's cool too and the solution my head of sales recommends.

What prize do I want to win?

7

GET GOOD AT LIFE, NOT JUST WORK

I'm tempted to continue ranting about overwork culture, but also, at this point in the book, perhaps I've said enough. Let's move forward, shall we? Let's dive in and swim around all the beauty of life we have yet to savor. All the parts we will refuse to concede!

From here on out we're going to march right out of the conference room, past the turnstiles logging badge swipes, and walk into the sunlight together. I hope I've convinced you it's worth defending your time from Excel and her culture of overwork. But it's not much fun if you don't use that reclaimed time for anything good. So in this chapter we're going to explore what it looks like to be a fairly productive but wildly happy human.

IN THIS CHAPTER

PUT YOUR TIME WHERE YOUR VALUES ARE

We are more than our output
....

PTO is just your life
....

Peak Life is not recharging
to do more work
....

Peak Life at CarMax
....

The joy of astonishment
....

New paths are everywhere
....

If you enjoy your time,
it's long enough
....

HOW TO GET GOOD AT LIFE

Unlearn learned helplessness
....

Live the life you want
....

Design your portfolio life
....

Be an "Exceeds
Expectations" human
....

Become an Ultimate Lounger
....

Do a thing just because you like it
....

Don't delay the fun
....

PUT YOUR TIME WHERE YOUR VALUES ARE

We are more than our output

We were at the beach one day when Brad said to a friend of ours, "It was so nice to have a day to do nothing." Our friend responded, "Nothing?! When was the last time you had lobster for lunch and swam so vigorously in the sea? You did everything!" Of course Brad was referring to having done no work—the measure of how productive we are for business or society.

Even though I think about this kind of thing for a living, I still find myself surprised at how the assumed primacy of work seeps into our thoughts, our language, our choices. It's infectious! And over time it brainwashes us to believe we are only as good as our outputs. That we are only *worth* our outputs.

How has the world managed to convince us we're no better than machines?

PTO is just your life

"How was your break?" is a sneaky line that graces countless Zoom rooms around January 2nd.

Thinking of time away from work as a break elevates our working lives to our primary, default mode as humans, and relegates time focused on ourselves, family, and friends as a time out, or secondary, intermittent mode. It assumes time off from work is for recharging our batteries, with the sole purpose of pushing harder when we get back to work.

In other words, is the zebra white with black stripes or black with white stripes? Is a break a stripe painted upon a life of work? Or is work layered upon the skin of our lives?

Candidly, I haven't figured out a better question to ask people about their "breaks." "How was your life?" sounds stupid and morbid. I've tried, "How was your time?" but then people are sometimes like, "What?" Suggestions welcome.

Peak Life is not recharging to do more work

Brad, Arden, and I travel with our friends Jenessa and Garrett every summer. Last year we did an Adriatic road trip, and one of our stops was on the Bay of Kotor in Montenegro.

There was a moment when I was sitting in a beach chair, looking out at Brad, with his *George of the Jungle* hair, bobbing in the waves on an over-sized blow-up flamingo float. Jenessa, who can inexplicably tread water indefinitely, was bobbing not far away. There I was on a beautiful day in a magical place with people I love. Do you ever feel like you want to take a mental Polaroid so you can live in a moment forever?

I was living Peak Life!

Which is a term we came up with for when you feel in your bones that it doesn't get any better than RIGHT NOW.

Note: That moment was *not* us recharging so that we may be better employees upon our return to work the following week.

Want to see?

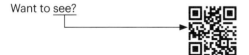

Peak Life at CarMax

I know, I know, I introduced the Peak Life idea with a vacation vignette, which might rouse Excel from her slumber to say, "And how do you think you *paid* for that vacation?"

So yes, that moment was absolutely Peak Life, but Peak Life is so much more complex and beautiful and nuanced than that.

About a month before my mom died I took my parents back to Chicago to gather things from their house that they wanted to bring to NYC. When I had first moved them earlier that year, it was such a whirlwind. I was trying to get my mom to her new oncologist as fast as humanly possible, so we packed up a few suitcases and left the house as is. One afternoon when we were back, I left my parents and their angel of a caregiver, Nini, at the house while I went to CarMax to sell their car.

After everything was sorted, I remember standing outside this suburban CarMax, waiting for an Uber to take me back to the house. I must have known somewhere in my bones that I wouldn't have my mom for much longer. I stood there with wave after wave of gratitude washing over me for the simple, mundane knowing that I could go home to my mom. Knowing it would not be true forever. But it was true now.

Peak Life.

The Joy of Astonishment

Me: What was unique about Milton?

Sue: I think it was his ability to be astonished throughout his life. Sometimes we would be working, and if I changed a color in a rug pattern, it was the most exciting thing to him.

In the words of Milton himself:

I think the most interesting thing that one can say about one's later life is that if you can sustain your interest in what you're doing, you're an extremely fortunate person ... You [can] sort of get tired and indifferent and sometimes defensive and you can lose your capacity for astonishment. And that's a great loss. Because the world is a very astonishing place. So I think what I feel fortunate about is that I am still astonished; that things still amaze me.
....

Don't we all want to feel astonished by the world? When was the last time you felt swept up in delight over the color in a rug? What makes me endlessly sad is to realize Milton was talking about later life as if that's when the ennui usually sets in. And yet how many people have lost the capacity for astonishment long before that? Have you? I know I have many times.

Fortunately, the world is an astonishing place and always will be.

It waits patiently for us to notice.

I wish there was
a way to know
you're in the
good old days before
you've actually
left them.

ANDY BERNARD, *The Office*

New paths are everywhere

When our NYC lease was up during the pandemic, we put everything in storage and tried being digital nomads. As it did for many, the pandemic made us reflect on why we were spending our life confined to a little white box.

The reason we felt brave enough to do this was because we knew it was possible. My friend Daniel Lombardi was a digital nomad with a family back in 2014 before it was cool. So we went.

When we were living in the English countryside during this time, I would walk through the bucolic forest preserve near us almost daily. I always walked the same path, to the same rock. For some reason I liked to tap my foot on that rock when I reached it before returning home. Walk. Tap. Walk. Home. Just like that. And then one day I tapped the rock, turned around, and saw an ENTIRE OTHER PATH leading from that rock that I had never noticed before.

Okay, maybe my story about a path and a rock is not as riveting as I hoped, but what I learned that day is this: *there are new paths everywhere if you look for them.*

My frequent collaborator Alice Katter spends her time expanding her incredible platform Out of Office, freelancing, writing, hosting residencies, and enjoying everything from rug-making classes to yoga retreats. Whenever I get an email from her, she signs it, "Hugs from sunny Barcelona/Tuscany/Vienna . . ."

My friend Hernán Carranza has been taking year-long mini-retirements throughout his life. In his most recent one, he stepped back from his role as chief innovation officer of Intercorp, Peru's largest conglomerate, and spent the year traveling with his family.

Another friend, Ian Sanders, has been working for himself for over 20 years. In the days I was burning out in back-to-backs, I would sometimes scroll LinkedIn and see a picture of him on a walk with a colleague or a picture of the lake he'd jumped in after the workshop he led. It's no surprise he wrote the gorgeous book *365 Ways to Have a Good Day*, which, fun fact, inadvertently includes 364 ways to have a good day. I would think to myself, "I think he's figured out something I haven't . . ."

Are these other paths available to everyone? Frankly, no. They require a degree of savings and tolerance for financial risk. They often require the absence of caregiving responsibilities and a good bit of privilege. They also require a lot of logistics. Those things may prevent someone from taking the other path. But far too often it's something else: the fear of trying a different kind of life. We blame the logistics and the unreasonableness of it all, convinced we simply don't have the power to take ourselves somewhere new, all while rocking these glittery red shoes that somehow got on our feet.

If you enjoy your time, it's long enough

Years ago in Tuscany I was talking with our Italian host-turned-lifelong-friend Gabriela. Arden was young, maybe two or three. Gabriela's kids were already in their early twenties. She said something sweet about Arden, and I doled out what I thought was some agreeable platitude like, "I know, it goes by too fast, doesn't it?"

"No," she said. Wait. *What?* I must have looked stunned and confused because she explained, "If you enjoy your time, it's long enough."

I think about that moment a lot. Have we anesthetized ourselves with busyness? Can we not feel all the richness and tiny, beautiful moments because we're always trying to finish "this one thing"? Have we lost the plot?

When we race to the end of the week, the quarter, the year, we also race to the end of our lives. Or in the words of the luminary Ferris Bueller, "Life moves pretty fast. If you don't stop and look around once in a while, you could miss it."

HOW TO GET GOOD AT LIFE

Unlearn learned helplessness

Famed psychologist Martin Seligman once ran an experiment to better understand the relationship between agency and depression. In the first phase, he placed dogs on a floor that gave their feet a slight electric shock. Some dogs were able to stop the shock by pressing a lever. Others were not and simply had to endure it.

In the second phase, those same dogs were placed in a crate with a divider. Half the crate floor was electrified and the other half was not. The dogs that were able to press the lever in the first phase knew the shocks weren't inevitable, looked for an out, and jumped over the small divider to the safe half of the crate. The dogs who were made to endure the shocks the first time simply laid down and whimpered. They had acquired what Dr. Seligman calls "learned helplessness." The only thing that helped the dogs break free from their acquiescence was the researchers picking up their paws and showing them how to walk away.

Too many people find themselves as the sad dog in that crate (or Zoom room, if you will). They believe that a stress-laden life is all that's on offer.

I write this from the other side of the crate.

I know I'm there when I take my dad on a walk instead of returning that email. When I prioritize my health over my productivity. When I'm snuggling Arden to sleep, thinking only of her and how lucky I am—and not the Slack I need to respond to. All while feeling genuine enjoyment and pride in the time I do spend working.

Come join me. The air is fine out here.

Live the life you want

Me: What did Milton figure out that others didn't?

Sue: He figured out how to live the life he wanted. He grew up in a one-bedroom apartment with a sister in the Bronx. He would say that they had nothing, but it felt like more than enough. He told me that he slept under a stove or something, which was common at that time. And from that he made the life that he wanted, which was full of making work that he felt good about, with people he liked, teaching thousands of students, and he was able to sustain his way financially. Of all things, that's what he really figured out.

....

How many of us never do!

Design your portfolio life

In the words of author Michael Bungay Stanier, "Your calendar tells you what is important to you. You can talk about values, jazz-hand yourself about priorities, but your calendar is a mirror to your actual priorities."

For a long time, mine said that I valued work a lot, then sleep, then my husband and daughter, then British reality TV, then exercise. I did not feel great about that. If you asked me what I did every day, I'd probably say, "I work and I come home." Have you been there, too? Maybe you're there now? Just like having all your savings in a single stock, it's risky. You're overexposed to the risks of work. A bad day at work is a bad day of life. Your sense of meaning and purpose is also dependent on work. And you don't even want to think about what a lay-off might mean.

Instead, I prefer #portfoliolife, a way of diversifying my joy, de-centering work, and getting to do things like getting good at crossword puzzles. I'll note that this idea is distinct from side hustle culture, in that this isn't about diversifying your income streams. It's about diversifying your joy.

The portfolio life exercise is a way to gut check whether you're putting your time where your values are, today. As different chapters of life come and go, so too will your life projects, like one of those age-adjusted retirement accounts. For example, if you have young kids and a full-time job, the portfolio might have to be "keep job" and "keep kids alive" for a few years. For better or for worse, that time won't be forever.

The thing I like about a portfolio life is that it's an alternative to the mindset that there's work and then there's everything else you can squeeze in after work takes its share. The other thing I like is that it's become much clearer to me when I have to say no to new projects. This is how I build a life I want to live, every day. Or in the words of Ryan Holiday, "Vacations are great, but do you know what's even greater? Building a life that you don't need to escape from."

Let me show you how this works.

Here's my portfolio of life projects:

1 Writing, speaking, consulting
2 Launching a book (which you're reading, so, success!)
3 Supporting and enjoying time with my dad
4 Getting good at being a swim parent for Arden (running her to practices; learning kid athlete nutrition)
5 Getting healthy (nerding out about health and longevity; exercising four to five times a week)

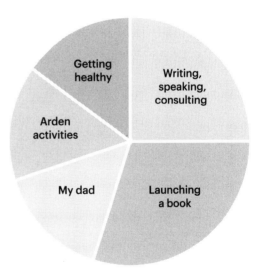

Note that I don't include things that I hope will be stable my whole life, like my marriage or friends or sleep. I tend to include active projects that I imagine will come or go in my life. In the case of getting healthy, while right now I'm actively learning about things like strength training, in the future I hope it will all become second nature and fall off my list of "active" portfolio projects.

Want to give it a go? Draw two circles side by side with dots in the middle of each. You're doing it right if it looks like boobs. Fill in the first with your current portfolio of projects. Then, if different, fill in the second with your ideal portfolio and compare.

What do you like about your portfolio today? What would you like to scale up or down? What's making a transition to your ideal portfolio hard? If a portfolio overhaul isn't feasible, are there some nudges you could make to your slices? After all, life is short, and we should enjoy our pie.

Be an "Exceeds Expectations" human

If you're an Above-and-Beyonder, then I know you like getting good at stuff. Excel will try to convince you that the most important thing to get good at is work. Chase that SVP title! Nail those OKRs! Grow that slice of pie! It can be addicting.

But it's not the only option for your A-student energy. There are other promotions to be had. Maybe you want the title of Super Parent or Gold Star Sleeper. It's great to be an "Exceeds Expectations" employee, but maybe it's just not as important as being an "Exceeds Expectations" human.

What title are you gunning for next?

Friend of the Month: Send a text to someone just to say something nice. Or send an old picture of you two. Or check in on how that thing they told you about is going.

Partner Extraordinaire: Write a cute note and put it on their pillow. Pick up something delicious and bring it to them. Tell them they look smokin' today. Think of a daily annoyance they live with (e.g., they can never find a charger) and fix it for them (e.g., buy them two more chargers and place them in strategic wall outlets).

Super Parent: Take your kid on an impromptu phone-free date. If you can swing it, make it a whole Week-of-Fun. Arden and I did a staycation week together that we filled with the New York Botanical Garden, MoMA, surfing lessons, making up our own exercise routine, and so much more. At the time it felt like a lot to plan and commit to the week, but it's one of my favorite weeks of my entire life.

Gold Star Sleeper: Everything is shitty when we're tired. Investing in good sleep is like grooming the goose that lays the golden eggs. There's so much to get nerdy about and experiment with here: room temperature, screens, things like magnesium and melatonin if that's your thing, and of course all the sleep trackers.

Committed Exerciser: Get that Stradivarius shining! What's great about exercise is that even if you're getting only a B in sleep and a C+ in nutrition, in the words of McMaster University professor Dr. Stuart Phillips, "Exercise forgives a lot of sins."

Exceedingly Happy Human: This can be anything from therapy and medication to making the recipe you love but never have time for, taking the scenic way home, or giving yourself time to cry or dance or do a little art.

And the best part is the head of the promotion committee for that last one is you!

Become an Ultimate Lounger

Jenessa and I coined the term "Ultimate Lounging" when we felt we were getting so good at relaxing, the Olympic committee might want to hear about it. As the name implies, Ultimate Lounging is the sport of extreme relaxation. Note that Ultimate Lounging is not to be confused with doom scrolling, which usually makes you feel like shit after. Ultimate Lounging makes you feel *great*.

How to plan some world-class Ultimate Lounging:

Make it intentional. You should tell your partner, a friend, or yourself, "It's Ultimate Lounging time!" This helps prevent the inadvertent doom scroll.

Make it comfortable for your body. This often involves pajamas, a bed/couch, fuzzy/heated/weighted blankets, a hot water bottle (my favorite), and maybe an open window if it's cool out so you get those "cuddled up" vibes.

Make it relaxing for your mind. You could do a puzzle or play a game, but to be honest, sometimes watching a screen is A+ lounging. I wouldn't recommend a war movie. Nor an audio meditation. In other words, nothing that will stress you out OR make you feel like you're doing something you "should" do. For me, the sweet spot is somewhere around *The Great British Bake Off* or the Never Too Small YouTube channel. But to each their own!

Make it delicious. I usually prefer something indulgent but not sickening, because who wants an Ultimate Lounging hangover? Popcorn, decent takeout, a delightful beverage—all good options.

Make it indefinite. Okay maybe not literally, but please don't try to Ultimate Lounge for 30 minutes before you have to make dinner. Think Saturday afternoon or a holiday. Just like a DND, our brains *revel* in being told, "Nothing to do, nowhere to go!"

Make it social. If you choose it to be. You can totally compete as an individual athlete. But it's time well spent if you want to try it with a friend, partner, child, or someone else. Extra points if you put your phone away.

You might be thinking, "Bree, turning relaxation into a sport is kind of intense..." and you would be right. If your brain is trying to tell you relaxation is lazy, it's a way you can tell it right back, "Is not! It's a competitive sport!" It's a strategy I've found effective, but there's also another way: do a thing just because you like it.

Do a thing just because you like it

There's a word to describe activities that you do simply for their own sake: atelic. The prefix *a* means "not," and the *telic* comes from telos in Greek, which means "end or goal." In other words, atelic means activities with no goal. They're things like going for a walk because it's fun and not because you need to get your steps in. The activity is the reward.

I haven't always been great at atelic activities. They used to feel almost *wrong.* Somehow, through education and culture and work and capitalism, I found myself conditioned to be constantly optimizing *something.* If I wasn't working, I was trying to improve my health, my relationships, or my home. It's why I used to be a terrible fiction reader. Is the only thing I'm going to get out of this ENJOYMENT? That doesn't sound right...

Anyway, that's how it used to go in my head. And sometimes I still have to whac-a-mole those thoughts back down.

You might be thinking, "Oh, I take vacations! And I exercise. And I read every day." But do you think of vacations as in service of your family? Exercise in service of your health? Reading in service of building your skills? If so, as wonderful as those things are, they are not atelic.

What I hope for you, for me, for every human on the planet, is that we all feel deserving of doing things JUST BECAUSE WE LIKE THEM. If I were the queen (of anything really), I would declare jigsaw puzzles a human right. Totally useless. All joy. And speaking of puzzles, I'm not sure if you enjoy a crossword as much as I do, but if so, want to take some time now away from all the thinking and reflecting and just... chill? Please enjoy this atelic activity, from me to you. If you get stuck, ask a friend. If you get really stuck, make something up! This is for fun, the whole fun, and nothing but the fun. You can find the solution in the back of the book. And once again, you are welcome to tear these pages out for ease of crosswording.

CROSSWORD BY JOHN M. SAMSON

ACROSS

1 Halloween wear
5 Kind of fund
10 Latin love
14 "Do _____ others as ..."
15 "_____ la vista!"
16 "_____ la France!"
17 Soccer score
18 Prime draftees
19 Part of DNA
20 A way to escape an uncomfortable dwelling
23 Suffix for progress
24 Tic-tac-toe winner
25 Peace Nobelist Nelson
29 50/50 proposition
33 Future oak
34 Put in the bank
36 Opposite of WSW
37 A smart acquisition before a holiday or leadership meeting
41 "Ready, _____, fire!"
42 Mr., in Munich
43 Tennis legend Chris
44 Cut off, culturally
47 Fairy-like creatures
49 _____ 'easter
50 Vehicle mileage indicator, briefly
51 An endurance athlete who's one to watch
60 Pelt-based apparel
61 Edited out, in publishing terms
62 Machu Picchu resident
63 Nabisco cookie
64 Painter's prop
65 "Memory" musical
66 Spotted
67 Satisfy a thirst
68 "Hold it right there!"

DOWN

1 Coffee cups
2 Endangered buffalo
3 Stick around
4 Yom Kippur prayer
5 Snow removal tool
6 London's Drury _____
7 Type of ID
8 ER "Now!"
9 Review in detail
10 King Arthur's paradise
11 Computer clickers
12 Sheep genus
13 Crimson hues
21 Newsworthy happening
22 Fair-hiring abbr.
25 Pastoral Kenyan people
26 Be a cast member
27 Typical patterns
28 Tribe of Israel
29 Civil-rights leader Medgar
30 "John Brown's Body" poet
31 _____ nous (between us)
32 Exams
35 Oxygen-rich mix
38 Pantomime game
39 Pain _____ (French French toast)
40 Aircraft electronic systems
45 Perfect harmony
46 _____o Saltado (Peruvian dish)
48 Labradoodle parent
51 Mystery airships
52 Carrot on a stick
53 Forest giant
54 Greenish blue
55 *Frozen* queen
56 Vichyssoise ingredient
57 Biting fly
58 Prefix meaning "outer"
59 Speak hoarsely

Fun fact: I grew up serving as a judge at the American Crossword Puzzle Tournament because my great aunt Helene is a professional puzzle constructor. Before I wrote this book, my great claim to literary fame was showing up as the love interest in a book about competitive crossword tournaments, *Crossworld* by Marc Romano.

Don't delay the fun

Sort of like never going to the tourist attractions in the place you live, sometimes it can feel like the fun things you always mean to do—the atelic joys—can be pushed off until someone comes to town or you retire. But that is not a good idea. Don't make me pull out all my existential dread again. I thought it might be better to go carrot this time, and so here we have a Fortune Teller! You can use it solo or with family and friends.

Okay, this is how it works:

1   Tear out the Fortune Teller on page 221 or use a blank square of paper.

2   Fold the Fortune Teller according to your eight-year-old self's instructions or follow <u>this QR code</u> for video instructions by me and Arden.

3   Use the list of sample fortunes (or make up your own!) to fill in the eight blank spaces. If you're doing this with others, pick the activities together.

4   Ask yourself, a friend, or a family member to choose a word from the flaps—Today, Was, Seriously, Fun. Move the Fortune Teller back and forth, spelling out the word.

5   Wherever you land, ask them to pick a number from inside. Move the Fortune Teller back and forth that many times.

6   Ask them to pick another number, and this time open the flap and read.

7   Do the thing! And enjoy yourself!

My mission in life
is not merely to
survive, but to thrive;
and to do so with
some passion,
some compassion,
some humor, and
some style.

MAYA ANGELOU

Sample fortunes

Pick the things that feel joyful, enlivening, or astonishing to you and anyone doing this with you. Write those things in the eight blanks in your Fortune Teller. I will warn you I'm a little nerdy, so you might have to add your own cooler things:

- Make a pizza and add highly unusual toppings (Pop Rocks, anyone?)
- Start a windowsill garden
- Make a playlist of songs that came out the year you were 18 years old
- Look through old family photos
- Have a picnic indoors or out
- Learn about naked mole rats
- Learn about harmonic series
- Go in search of the best donut you can find and eat it
- Get under the covers and read a book for two hours
- Go to three different restaurants that have your favorite appetizer and rate them (We did this with Arden for French onion soup and it was so fun. She created her own rating system for the bread, cheese, and the broth. FWIW, the Odeon in NYC won.)
- Take turns giving each other a back massage (obv, choose this one depending on the audience; NSFW)
- Play Twister! (samesies)
- Try sitting still, quietly, and just looking around the room for five minutes straight
- Find the nearest jazz show and get tickets
- Take yourself on a field trip to a museum of your choice, by yourself
- Lie down, close your eyes, and listen to a podcast about something you know nothing about

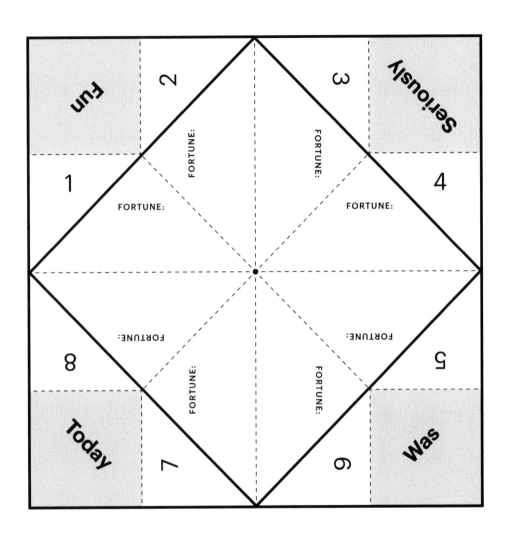

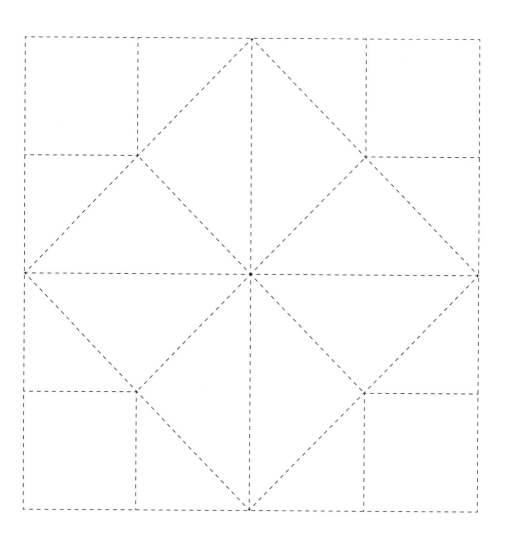

Oh, hello. Did you just read the whole section and not make the Fortune Teller or anything? If you made it and did a thing, you have my respect and excitement for you! If you didn't, well, I have been there, my friend. "Yeah yeah, these seem like activities someone does, but not really me. Maybe I'll come back to it later." But as they say, if nothing changes, nothing changes. I dare you to pick one and do it RIGHT NOW. YOU WON'T REGRET IT. OR AT LEAST PLAN IT. I AM YELLING AT YOU.

Nearly two decades ago when I was teaching, one of our professional development assignments was to go to a museum of our choice by ourselves for the day. I went to LACMA in LA, and to this day that was one of the most astonishing days of my entire life. I wandered around with no agenda amidst all this beauty and imagination and it was glorious. What did it take to get me there? Someone had to make me. So I'll return the favor: PICK A THING FROM THE LIST. DO IT. NOT OPTIONAL.

To change one's life:

1 *Start immediately.*
2 *Do it flamboyantly.*
3 *No exceptions.*

Attributed to William James.

Closing thought

Life is art, not performance.
Life is joy, not endurance.
Life is play, not production.

This life is no dress rehearsal. When a day passes, it does not come back again. And if you're going to spend your days getting good at anything, I think it should be life!

PARTING THOUGHTS

We spend a third of our lives at work.
Our lives should be fun.
Ergo, work should be fun.

To me, it's that simple.

Some might argue it's not about us, the employees; that it's about the impact, the customers, the results; that employees are just inputs to the system. But that's never sat right with me. I fully understand that it's the customers that bring the money and make the business run—of course we need to care about them, and I dare say caring about them is part of the fun! But ultimately, a customer is giving a share of their wallet. An employee is giving a grand portion of their life. They're giving time away from family and friends and the sum of their professional skills. And they're often sacrificing their health and sleep for the job, too.

But more than that, they're not "they." They're us! Bob's shaking his head at us because it's we, the humans, who have made work what it is today. There are loads of reasons why this is, most of them pertaining to power and money, but it simply is not fundamentally true that it must be this way. We can make it different.

So what should it be instead?

There is no shortage of articles, books, and consultants in the world trying to figure this out. And I have loads of respect for the experts out there writing about the nuances of employee benefits, decision-making frameworks, and feedback processes. But it's hard to make things better if we don't first share an underlying philosophy of what work should even *be*: the role it should play in our lives, what it should feel like when we're doing it, and what end it serves.

I love a good evocative chapter title that includes notions of stretchy pants and shoveling shit, but if we strip all that away, the core philosophy is simple:

1 Work should be fun

2 It should feel human

3 We should do it with friends

4 And make brilliant things

5 With a sense of perspective

6 As one joyful part

7 Of a big, beautiful life

Everything else is accoutrement.

I hope you'll take away a newfound sense of what work can be (or oldfound, if you're like, "Bree, I agreed from page 1!"). I also hope you'll take away stories that you'll retell, phrases that will magically pop to mind when you need them (Nevertheless!), and some tools you can use in your day-to-day.

I can't help but include one more interactive page to give you space to organize your thinking about what you want to take forward. First, you'll find a list of every segment in the book, and I invite you to reflect back and circle the ones that stood out to you. Then, you'll find a prompt: What is one thing—an idea, a quote, a story—that you'll take away with you above all else? If you're up for it, give it a go now.

Today was good.
Today was fun.
Tomorrow is
another one.

DR. SEUSS

5. Keep it cool—we're all in it together · Fun requires emotional reliability
Emotionally reliable leaders do three things · Your emotions are
contagious · **Don't eliminate your emotions, domesticate them** · People
who lost their shit and didn't lose their shit: Ernest Hemingway · **People
who lost their shit and didn't lose their shit: My mom** · If you keep it
cool, you can stay in the fire · **Optimism in the face of shit** · It all passes
Shout: "NEVERTHELESS!" · Ask: Are we in Corsica? · **Be the narrator of
your team** · Conduct a pre-mortem

PART TWO: ... ONE OF MANY IN OUR LIVES

**6. You are the defender of date nights, crossword puzzles, and
your health** · Work is addicting · **Delayed gratification is overrated**
The perils of above and beyond · **Purpose is alluring** · Your bones will
tell you where to be · **Excel doesn't care if you live or die** · Dread by
the numbers · **Bob has seen enough** · Not busy is possible · Understand
the psychology of overwork · **Ask yourself: Do I want that prize?** · Know
who gets the best of you · **Make people whole** · Detox your belief system
Detox your behaviors

7. Get good at life, not just work · We are more than our output · **PTO is
just your life** · Peak Life is not recharging to do more work · **Peak Life at
CarMax** · The joy of astonishment · **New paths are everywhere** · If you
enjoy your time, it's long enough · Unlearn learned helplessness · **Live the
life you want** · Design your portfolio life · **Be an "Exceeds Expectations"
human** · Become an Ultimate Lounger · **Do a thing just because you like it**
Don't delay the fun

What is one thing—an idea, a quote, a story—that you'll take away with you above all else? Write or sketch below.

It's been an honor to write this book, and I'm so grateful you spent some of your finite time reading it. I hope we'll stay in touch. You can find me at my website breegroff.com, on Substack @breegroff, and on LinkedIn. I'm chuckling thinking of my great grandchildren finding this book and wondering what the hell a LinkedIn is and why I didn't include my hologram handle. Hello, great grandkids! I hope you too are finding life big and beautiful.

Sending you off with one last story, and all my good wishes for more fun days:

I shared that when I learned of my mom's cancer diagnosis, I decided I had one strategy, and that was to leave all of my love on the table. That was my first instinct: pour it all out.

But my second instinct was this: soak it all in.

I refused to wait for the second marshmallow. I wanted to save my mom, yes, but that was not for me to do. My job was to savor her: her text messages with four exclamation points and the way she always signed her cards with an XO followed by a heart, smiley face, and little paw prints; the way everything felt right when my heart was next to her heart, like my body knew she was my first home.

Bank it, I told myself. Bank the joy, the peace, the happiness. Bank it now. Feel every corner of every glorious second. Put it away like a squirrel saving for a rainy day.

It was so immediate, so visceral what I needed to do. I was on the clock.

Except I still am.
As are you.
We share the same terminal disease.
I myself may have only 40 or 50 years left.

And therefore, the same strategies apply: *Pour it all out. Soak it all in.*

Play this song:

Start today!

Dear Andy: Congratulations on your thirtieth anniversary with Ace Hardware. I'm sure it seems like you started just yesterday, but then time goes fast when you are having fun.

ROGER E. PETERSON, vice president operations, Ace Hardware Corporation, written to my grandfather, Andrew Hovanec, on May 7, 1984

ACKNOWLEDGEMENTS

My mom always insisted I write thank you letters after receiving a gift, so I think I got pretty good at them. But given this text will exist forever in the world, it's definitely my highest-stakes note!

First, let me share my gratitude to the big-hearted and formidably talented Page Two team. To Jesse, Page Two's co-founder, from our first meeting I knew I wanted to be in your capable hands. To Peter and the Page Two design team, I'm so grateful for your support in bringing these words to life through design. To Tass, my project manager, thank you for keeping the whole process full of ease and joy. You have the patience of 10 pre-school teachers and the organizational skills of a NASA launch director, and I'm so grateful for your work in bringing this book to life. To Adrineh, my proofreader, you are as eagle-eyed as they come. This book shines like a freshly polished Ferrari because of you—thank you. To Jenny, my copyeditor, thank you for keeping my writing tight and my endnotes fun! Or as fun as endnotes can be... Your passion for grammar and style guides is delightful, and you've taught me so much. To my editor, Sarah, you are uncommonly thoughtful. Dear reader, there is a LOT of blabbing on the cutting room floor that, because of Sarah's edits, you don't have uselessly bopping around your brain. Sarah, you kept me honest, kept me sharp, and most of all kept me laughing. Your squeees made me "Squeee!" Thank you for being my partner in creating this book. I could not have asked for a better one. You are an exceptional editor, but also you are an exceptional human, and I had so much fun working with you. Shall we do it again once this book is a grand success and the world needs another?!

I am so lucky to have luminary collaborators in my corner. To my cover designers Rodrigo Corral, Anna Corral, and the whole studio team: you are the embodiment of chapter 4. I am endlessly proud to have your art on this cover. To Melisa Goldie, my former client who knows there's no such thing as a fashion emergency, thank you for your encouragement and friendship and for supporting the launch of this book with your inimitable marketing instincts.

To Dini, thank you for being the creative force behind my murder scene. To Derrick, thank you for letting me ask your opinion on the book 10,000 times. If anyone reading this needs a photographer or book doula, respectively, I know some guys.

To Nick Morgan, my speaking coach and the person who first gave me the confidence and skills to stand on a stage, thank you. You inspired me to see that a book could be more than a tool to communicate or a credential. Instead, it could be a way to be part of the story of humanity—a way to carve my name into the tree of life with a little "Bree was here."

To Avi Shernoff, my executive coach and dear friend, thank you for always knowing exactly what my creative soul needs. You center me, buoy me, and make me feel like the world is my oyster. This book was written by the garden fairy.

To Sue, thank you for being my friend, my collaborator, and the fountain of so much inspiration. I love how dedicated you are to the things that make you feel alive. I love that you see miracles everywhere. And I am so grateful for the way you share your relationship with Milton with me and the world. Your stories of Milton have made this book so much richer. I can't wait for the day you write your book about your experience working with Milton. The world is waiting! And to Shirley and Milton's estate, I am forever grateful that you've allowed me to be one more conduit for Milton's brilliance and wisdom.

While so many contributed to the book itself, it also wouldn't be possible without all the humans who supported me and my ability to write it. Think Coffee and Bluestone Lane, thank you for letting me overstay my welcome and for the dozens of avocado toasts and protein mocha smoothies. Inness, thank you for hosting me as I churned out thousands of words at my writer's retreat, and thank you to one kind server who was the first person to ask me if I was a writer, and I got to say yes! Forward Space and Hanson Fitness, thank you for all the sweat and joy and keeping my Stradivarius singing.

And finally, to my family and friends: I love you.

To Nini, who first took care of my mom and dad, thank you for being the angel that you are. You were there for my mom in the end, and I can't thank you enough for making her days joyful and full of laughs. For her, you were the definition of good laughs with good people.

To Lika, my dad's caregiver, you are like the sister I never had. As an only child, I can't tell you how profound it feels to be able to lean on someone to take care of my dad. You have the absolute highest standards for his health and happiness, and the best part is, although he can be a handful, you seem to do it all with so much joy and lightness. The way you dance with him every day. The way you cook for him with such love. I love you dearly, and I will be forever grateful to you.

To Lizzie and Jenessa, thank you for being my lifelong friends. Lizzie, you are unapologetically yourself in all times and all places, which has taught me to do the same. You are the reason I show up at work as Bree and tell my colleagues about my bad hair days and favorite reality TV. You're also the reason I let the unapologetic voice in my head hold the pen in these pages. Jenessa, you have been my partner in seeing this beautiful world and so many moments of Peak Life. The way you supported me with such wisdom and love when I was supporting my mom is the reason I can write about that time with any sense of peace and perspective.

To the parental figures in my life, I know if they could, my parents would like to say, "Thank you for looking out for Bree." To Jack and Judy (Lizzie's parents), you've always made me feel that I had another home in Maryland—one filled with love and support and really good lox cream cheese. You've been there for me from the first day we met in the dorms and you found me organizing my tank tops by color, through to every big life event I've seen in the 20+ years since then. Thank you for staying close all that time. To Patty and Walt (my in-laws), thank you for making Brad! I know I won the in-law lottery every time we enjoy a delicious meal at your home with holiday-themed plates, every time Arden runs to you both with a big hug and adoration in her eyes, and in all the moments you support Brad and me in ways big and small. And after two incredibly meaningful careers, to see you travel the world with friends and delight in your grandchildren and swim and golf and play tennis and bridge, it all makes me think: I want to be like you when I grow up! You sure have gotten good at life.

To my grandparents, thank you for showing me from an early age that life could be fun. Grandma Vera and Grandpa Harold, wherever I go I carry with me the memory of the scent of lilacs next to the pond where you and I would go to feed the ducks, enjoying the life of a "fisherman." Grandma Olga, you and I were the queens of atelic activities. We'd busy ourselves handmaking puffy bows for presents, adding electricity to my dollhouse, and sneaking midnight snacks. Grandpa Andy, thank you for teaching me how to garden and make perfect scrambled eggs. You taught me about the joy of everyday life, and also the joy of work. I still remember the collage your colleagues put together for you when you retired, just dripping with humanity and camaraderie and fun. I still have your work nameplate at my desk as a reminder to show up with your brand of brilliance and ease.

To my mom and dad, how I wish you both could read this book. Dad, you have given me everything. I feel your love for me so deeply, and although teenage me might be shocked, I love every minute I spend with you these days. Every one. You have taught me how to soak it all in. Mom, I think if you knew I had written a book, you would say, "You never cease to amaze me!" and I would glow in the warmth of your love and pride and never want to leave. I love you as much as a child can love.

To Brad, when I first told you I wanted to write a book, you looked at me like it was the most sensible thing in the world. Thank you for never once doubting that I could do it. You inspire me in so many ways: your dedication to learning just for fun, the way we can never leave a new country we've traveled to without you trying to figure out how we might live there, and the way you share your ideas and interests with Arden. And since we've collaborated on many a life project, I think I can say: you are my all-time favorite coworker. I love you, and also, I just like hanging around you.

To Arden, you've given me the best days. I loved the day I took you to work with me and you flew paper airplanes with Dini. I loved the day we went to the Botanical Garden and rode the tram in the rain and the squirrel stole your grilled cheese. I've even loved the days when things were hard, simply because you were there. You have the biggest heart and fiercest spirit of anyone I've ever known, and though I have no doubt you have all sorts of successes and accolades ahead of you, what I wish most for you is this:

A lifetime of curling up in bed at night and thinking:

Today was fun.

ALL THE ANSWERS

M	A	S	K		S	L	U	S	H		A	M	O	R
U	N	T	O		H	A	S	T	A		V	I	V	E
G	O	A	L		O	N	E	A	S		A	C	I	D
S	A	Y	N	E	V	E	R	T	H	E	L	E	S	S
			I	V	E			O	O	O				
M	A	N	D	E	L	A		E	V	E	N	B	E	T
A	C	O	R	N		S	A	V	E		E	N	E	
S	T	R	E	T	C	H	I	E	R	P	A	N	T	S
A	I	M			H	E	R	R		E	V	E	R	T
I	N	S	U	L	A	R		S	P	R	I	T	E	S
			N	O	R			O	D	O				
U	L	T	I	M	A	T	E	L	O	U	N	G	E	R
F	U	R	S		D	E	L	E	D		I	N	C	A
O	R	E	O		E	A	S	E	L		C	A	T	S
S	E	E	N		S	L	A	K	E		S	T	O	P

I hope you had a great time!

NOTES

Chapter 1

p. 14   *"How we spend our days"*: Annie Dillard, *The Writing Life* (Harper Perennial, 1990).

p. 20   *the value you get from your job*: Dart Lindsley is not only an expert on the topic of humanity at work but also a friend of mine. So I definitely think you should get your hands/ears on more of his brilliant insights at dartlindsley.com/work-for-humans-podcast.

p. 21   *Michael: "All he does is work"*: *Elf*, directed by Jon Favreau (New Line Cinema, 2003).

p. 24   *organizations such as Starbucks and Pfizer*: Starbucks, "Mission & Values," careers .starbucks.com/culture/mission-and-values; Pfizer, "Our Purpose," pfizer.com/about/ purpose.

p. 25   *"I can't get enough dinosaurs!"*: "The One with Christmas in Tulsa," *Friends*, Season 9, Episode 10, 2002, but also here: Friends Addiction (@Friends_Addictionn), Instagram, April 10, 2024, instagram.com/friends_addictionn/reel/C5kk9oIrMhR.

p. 26   *"I'm helping to put a man on the moon"*: Jitske M.C. Both-Nwabuwe, Maria T.M. Dijkstra, and Bianca Beersma, "Sweeping the Floor or Putting a Man on the Moon: How to Define and Measure Meaningful Work," *Frontiers in Psychology* 8 (2017): 1658, doi.org/10.3389/fpsyg.2017.01658.

p. 29   *"You really want an answer?"*: John Leland, "Milton Glaser Still Hearts New York," *New York Times*, July 31, 2016, nytimes.com/2016/07/31/nyregion/milton-glaser-still-hearts-new-york.html.

p. 31   *"20 years from now, the only people"*: From the Reddit thread r/antiwork, posted by u/salinungatha, June 13, 2012, reddit.com/r/antiwork/comments/12uz90c/ psa_20_years_from_now_the_only_people_who_will.

p. 31   *"The Roman poet Juvenal joked"*: I highly recommend Ryan Holiday's newsletter and all of his books. Ryan Holiday, "It's Cheap to Be Dead," *Daily Stoic*, dailystoic.com/ its-cheap-to-be-dead.

p. 32   *"Go, even though there is nowhere to go"*: Cheryl Strayed speaks to my soul, and she might just speak to yours, too. Cheryl Strayed, "Dear Sugar, *The Rumpus* Advice Column #77: The Truth That Lives There," *The Rumpus*, June 24, 2011, therumpus .net/2011/06/24/dear-sugar-the-rumpus-advice-column-77-the-truth-that-lives-there.

p. 33   *"God, grant me the serenity"*: Laurie Goodstein, "Serenity Prayer Stirs Up Doubt: Who Wrote It?" *New York Times*, July 11, 2008, nytimes.com/2008/07/11/us/11prayer.html.

p. 34   *"You are not going to work"*: Apoorva Mandavilli, "Kati Kariko Helped Shield the World from the Coronavirus," *New York Times*, April 8, 2021, nytimes.com/2021/04/08/health/coronavirus-mrna-kariko.html.

p. 35   *"The qualities of vitality, curiosity, and spontaneity"*: Esther Perel, "Letters from Esther #17: Eroticism Suffered in 2020; Fantasy Thrived," EstherPerel.com, January 15, 2021, estherperel.com/blog/letters-from-esther-17-eroticism-suffered-fantasy-thrived.

p. 40   *"You can mark your progress breath by breath"*: Cheryl Strayed, "Dear Sugar, *The Rumpus* Advice Column #76: The Woman Hanging on the End of a Line," The Rumpus, June 16, 2011, therumpus.net/2011/06/16/dear-sugar-the-rumpus-advice-column-76-the-woman-hanging-on-the-end-of-a-line.

Chapter 2

p. 47   *Milton also had some thoughts about professionalism*: Sue Walsh, in conversation with the author, March 6, 2024.

p. 48   *the absurdity of the business costume*: Betabrand, "The Iconic DPYP," betabrand.com/collections/dress-pant-yoga-pants; Lambert Varias, "Executive Pinstripe Hoodie," theawesomer.com/executive-pinstripe-hoodie/168615.

p. 49   *Interviewer: "Do you think of yourself as a style icon?"*: "10 Things Jerry Seinfeld Can't Live Without," posted May 1, 2024, by GQ, YouTube, youtube.com/watch?v=YL2sr99Sv18.

p. 51   *According to a survey from Indeed*: Emma Burleigh, "Some Black Workers Say if They Stopped Code Switching at Work It Would Hurt Their Careers," *Fortune*, February 1, 2024, fortune.com/2024/02/01/black-workers-code-switching-burden-indeed.

p. 52   *"the owner of one high-end men's clothing store"*: Vanessa Friedman, "Will the Tie Ever Make a Comeback?" *New York Times*, November 13, 2023, nytimes.com/2023/11/13/style/tie-necktie-fashion.html.

p. 56   *"I admire women who look"*: Vanessa Friedman, "What Does It Mean to 'Dress Your Age'?" *New York Times*, December 25, 2023, nytimes.com/2023/12/25/style/women-fashion-age-appropriate.html.

p. 58   *the concept of "dopamine dressing"*: Fiona also works at Forward Space, the dance/music/wellness/sweat studio in NYC that is responsible for, like, 80 percent of my mental and physical health. Fiona Harvey, LinkedIn, October 2024, linkedin.com/posts/fiona-harvey-mph-23620032_wellness-tv-publichealth-activity-7246527244066590720-xeEO.

p. 59   *"Surgeons are often listening to music in the OR"*: Peter Attia, "AMA #59: Inflammation: Its Impact on Aging and Disease Risk, and How to Identify, Prevent, and Reduce It," *Peter Attia*, May 13, 2024, peterattiamd.com/ama59.

Chapter 3

p. 63 Chapter title: Credit to my brilliant friend and mentor, Shannan Schuster, who said to me one day, "I could shovel shit for a living with the right people."

p. 67 *Work is something we do while we're hanging out on the planet*: Credit to my friend Jenessa for describing work this way to me. It's stuck!

p. 72 *BetterUp surveyed 1,400 full-time US employees*: Chase Peterson-Withorn, "Employees Are Spending the Equivalent of a Month's Grocery Bill on the Return to the Office—and Growing More Resentful Than Ever, New Survey Finds," *Fortune*, February 1, 2024, fortune.com/2024/02/01/employees-spending-equivalent-months-grocery-bill-return-to-office-resentful-survey.

p. 72 *Gallup found that commutes of only 30 minutes*: Jim Harter, "Why the Commute?" *Gallup*, May 1, 2023, gallup.com/workplace/474482/why-commute.aspx.

p. 73 *"The quality of your relationships"*: "Esther Perel: The Quality of Your Relationships Determines the Quality of Your Life," posted February 12, 2019, by Summit, YouTube, youtube.com/watch?v=LmDPAOE5V2Y.

p. 75 *Gallup has produced some impressive research*: Alok Patel and Stephanie Plowman, "The Increasing Importance of a Best Friend at Work," *Gallup*, August 17, 2022, gallup.com/workplace/397058/increasing-importance-best-friend-work.aspx.

p. 78 *just 12 percent of leaders say they have full confidence*: "Transforming Microsoft with Microsoft Teams: Collaborating Seamlessly, Teaming Up Fearlessly," Microsoft Inside Track, microsoft.com/insidetrack/blog/transforming-microsoft-with-microsoft-teams-collaborating-seamlessly-teaming-up-fearlessly.

p. 82 *"Breaks my heart that pirates"*: Jason Lastname (@JasonLastname), X, February 15, 2013, x.com/JasonLastname/status/302583665035206657.

p. 86 *leadership development is a $366 billion global industry*: Chris Westfall, "Leadership Development Is a $366 Billion Industry: Here's Why Most Programs Don't Work," *Forbes*, June 20, 2019, forbes.com/sites/chriswestfall/2019/06/20/leadership-development-why-most-programs-dont-work.

p. 87 *this relevant post made me guffaw*: Kristen Mulrooney (@MissMulrooney), X, June 26, 2021, x.com/missmulrooney/status/1408784392307331075.

p. 92 *This concept comes from child development specialist*: Harvey Karp, "Use the 'Fast-Food Rule' to Deal with an Upset Toddler," *Happiest Baby*, happiestbaby.com/blogs/toddler/how-to-talk-to-kids-when-upset-angry.

Chapter 4

p. 97 *watched a video of Taylor Swift talking about*: "Taylor Swift Tells Us How She Wrote 'Lover': Diary of a Song," posted December 24, 2019, by The New York Times, YouTube, youtube.com/watch?v=UEeWmltgdxA.

p. 101 *Greg McKeown... articulates this perfectly*: Greg McKeown, *Effortless: Make It Easier to Do What Matters Most* (Currency, 2021), 29.

p. 103 *"Lack of sleep leads to detriments in job performance"*: Tomas Chamorro-Premuzic, "How Much Is Bad Sleep Hurting Your Career?" *Harvard Business Review*, July 27, 2020, hbr.org/2020/07/how-much-is-bad-sleep-hurting-your-career.

p. 103 *"sleep-deprived leaders tend to be less charismatic"*: Christopher M. Barnes, "Research: Sleep-Deprived Leaders Are Less Inspiring," *Harvard Business Review*, June 15, 2016, hbr.org/2016/06/research-sleep-deprived-leaders-are-less-inspiring.

p. 105 *"There are three responses to a piece of design"*: "'Yes,' 'No,' and 'WOW!' of the Legendary Milton Glaser," 3DW Creative Digital Agency, July 8, 2020, https://3dworld.com.ua/en/yes-no-and-wow-of-the-legendary-milton-glaser.

p. 107 *"There is a vitality, a life force, an energy"*: Maria Popova, "Martha Graham on the Life-Force of Creativity and the Divine Dissatisfaction of Being an Artist," *The Marginalian*, October 2, 2015, themarginalian.org/2015/10/02/martha-graham-creativity-divine-dissatisfaction.

p. 112 *"I don't know. I've never seen anyone else"*: Keith Johnstone, *Impro: Improvisation and the Theater* (Routledge, 1987), 69.

p. 113 *A film critic told the story of what he saw*: Johnstone, *Impro*.

p. 114 *"Creative work is not a selfish act"*: Steven Pressfield, *The War of Art: Break Through the Blocks and Win Your Inner Creative Battles* (Black Irish Entertainment LLC, 2012), 165.

p. 115 *Cal Newport . . . calls this "Solitude Deprivation"*: Cal Newport, *Digital Minimalism: Choosing a Focused Life in a Noisy World* (Portfolio, 2019), 103.

p. 118 *"Doing something unimportant well"*: Timothy Ferriss, *The Four-Hour Work Week: Escape 9–5, Live Anywhere, and Join the New Rich* (Harmony Books, 2009), 70.

p. 120 *"97 percent of leaders say"*: Dorie Clark, "If Strategy Is So Important, Why Don't We Make Time for It?" *Harvard Business Review*, June 28, 2018, hbr.org/2018/06/if-strategy-is-so-important-why-dont-we-make-time-for-it.

p. 120 *"Employees spend 32 percent of their time"*: Amber Burton and Paolo Confino, "How Much Time Employees Say They Waste Trying to Look Busy," *Fortune*, May 4, 2023, fortune.com/2023/05/04/employees-waste-time-looking-busy-productivity.

p. 123 *"The best work is the work you are excited about"*: Rick Rubin, *The Creative Act: A Way of Being* (Penguin Press, 2023), 347.

p. 123 *"The more scared we are of a work or calling"*: *The War of Art* is one of the reasons I had the confidence to write this book. Steven Pressfield, *The War of Art: Break Through the Blocks and Win Your Creative Battles* (Black Irish Entertainment, 2002), 40.

p. 126 *"The goal isn't efficiency"*: Ed Catmull, quoted in Jenny Blake, "257: How to Become a Friction Fixer with Huggy Rao," *Free Time*, January 9, 2024, itsfreetime.substack.com/p/257.

p. 127 *"Only those thoughts that come by walking"*: Friedrich Nietzsche, *Twilight of the Idols*, trans. Anthony M. Ludovici (T.N. Foulis, 1911), 6.

p. 127   *creative output increases by an average of 60 percent*: May Wong, "Stanford Study Finds Walking Improves Creativity," *Stanford Report*, April 24, 2014, news.stanford .edu/stories/2014/04/walking-vs-sitting-042414.

p. 128   *"It is enough for me to sit back in my chair"*: I love that Agatha Christie always described Poirot's head as being egg-shaped but has said that she herself doesn't know which way up the egg was. She just knew it was egg-shaped and that was enough. "Quotes from Hercule Poirot," Agatha Christie (website), August 2, 2018, agathachristie.com/news/2018/eight-quotes-from-hercule-poirot.

p. 130   *"To see takes time"*: "Georgia O'Keeffe: To See Takes Time," Museum of Modern Art, New York, April 9 – August 12, 2023, moma.org/calendar/exhibitions/5493.

Chapter 5

p. 142   *"the wider range of feelings we can regulate"*: Becky Kennedy, "Parents: Don't Focus on Happiness, Help Build Resilience Instead," *Big Think*, October 29, 2022, bigthink .com/neuropsych/parents-dont-focus-on-happiness.

p. 144   *Behavioral psychologist Dr. Albert Mehrabian showed that*: Nick Morgan, "Debunking the Debunkers: The Mehrabian Myth Explained (Correctly)," *Public Words*, July 23, 2009, publicwords.com/2009/07/23/debunking-the-debunkers-the-mehrabian-myth-explained-correctly.

p. 144   *"a non-anxious presence," a concept originally coined*: Angela S. Hornsby, "Leadership as a Non-anxious Presence," *Lighthouse Resource Group*, lighthouseresourcegroup .com/leadership-as-a-non-anxious-presence.

p. 146   *"I have come to a frightening conclusion"*: Haim G. Ginott, *Teacher and Child: A Book for Parents and Teachers* (Macmillan, 1972), 15.

p. 147   *As Nassim Taleb says, "Stoicism is about"*: "How to Tame Negative Emotions," *Daily Stoic*, dailystoic.com/how-to-tame-negative-emotions.

p. 149   *In a letter to a friend, he wrote*: "Hemingway's Lost Suitcase," *Lost Manuscripts*, July 31, 2010, lostmanuscripts.com/2010/07/31/hemingways-lost-suitcase.

p. 153   *"And this, too, shall pass away"*: "This Too Shall Pass," Wikipedia, en.wikipedia.org/ wiki/This_too_shall_pass.

p. 153   *"If it's endurable, then endure it"*: "A Stoic Response to Complaining," *Daily Stoic*, dailystoic.com/a-stoic-response-to-complaining.

p. 155   *In 41 AD, the emperor Claudius banished Seneca*: D. Reynolds Dudley, "Seneca," *Encyclopedia Britannica*, July 27, 2024, britannica.com/biography/Lucius-Annaeus-Seneca-Roman-philosopher-and-statesman.

p. 157   *In hard times, urging people to stay positive*: Adam Grant, "Beyond Toxic Positivity," Adam Grant's Substack, February 11, 2024, adamgrant.substack.com/p/beyond-toxic-positivity.

p. 158 *"greater diversity in a team's trait positive affect"*: Sigal G. Barsade and Donald E. Gibson, "Group Affect: Its Influence on Individual and Group Outcomes," *Current Directions in Psychological Science* 21, no. 2 (2012): 119–123, doi.org/10.1177/0963721412438352.

p. 160 *"Prospective hindsight . . . increases the ability to correctly identify"*: Gary Klein, "Performing a Project Premortem," *Harvard Business Review*, September 2007, hbr.org/2007/09/performing-a-project-premortem.

Chapter 6

p. 168 *"How many have laid waste to your life"*: Seneca, *On the Brevity of Life*, 3.3b, trans. Stephen Hanselman, in Ryan Holiday, *The Daily Stoic: 366 Meditations on Wisdom, Perseverance, and the Art of Living* (Portfolio, 2016), 11.

p. 171 *the famous marshmallow experiment*: Walter Mischel and Ebbe B. Ebbeson, "Attention in Delay of Gratification," *Journal of Personality and Social Psychology* 16, no. 2 (1970): 329–337, psycnet.apa.org/doi/10.1037/h0029815.

p. 172 *"We are very good at preparing to live"*: Thich Nhat Hanh, *Peace Is Every Step: The Path of Mindfulness in Everyday Life* (Random House, 1992), 5.

p. 174 *"We shouldn't just work less"*: Simone Stolzoff, "A Better Argument for Working Less," Every, April 24, 2023, https://every.to/p/a-better-argument-for-working-less.

p. 179 *around 50 percent of people who experience*: Peter Attia, "AMA 34: What Causes Heart Disease?" *Peter Attia*, April 18, 2022, peterattiamd.com/ama34.

p. 180 *poor diet, physical inactivity, lack of sleep*: T.J. van Trier et al., "Lifestyle Management to Prevent Atherosclerotic Cardiovascular Disease: Evidence and Challenges," *Netherlands Heart Journal* 30, no. 1 (2022): 3–14, doi.org/10.1007/s12471-021-01642-y.

p. 180 *According to the American Institute of Stress*: "Workplace Stress," American Institute of Stress, stress.org/workplace-stress.

p. 181 *workforce attitudes toward mental health report*: Paige McGlauflin and Joseph Abrams, "Nearly Half of Employees Say They Dread Coming to Work at Least Once a Week," *Fortune*, August 22, 2023, fortune.com/2023/08/22/headspace-workforce-mental-health-report-employee-dread.

p. 181 *Henry Ford standardized a five-day workweek*: "40-Hour Work Week: Its History and Future," *ActiPLANS* (blog), actiplans.com/blog/40-hour-work-week.

p. 181 *89 percent of employees surveyed*: McGlauflin and Abrams, "Nearly Half of Employees."

p. 182 *On your computer, open Google Calendar*: "Create an Event in Google Calendar," Google Support, support.google.com/calendar/answer/72143.

p. 190 *"If it matters, make time for it"*: Ian Sanders, "I'm an Optimism Coach with Cancer—Here's How I Stay Positive," *The i Paper*, August 24, 2024, https://inews.co.uk/inews-lifestyle/optimism-coach-cancer-stay-positive-3237422.

p. 193 *"Women don't step back from work"*: Claire Cain Miller, "Women Did Everything Right. Then Work Got 'Greedy,'" *New York Times*, April 26, 2019, nytimes.com/2019/04/26/upshot/women-long-hours-greedy-professions.html.

p. 195 *"Perhaps I'm just getting old, but my definition"*: Tim Ferriss (@TFerriss), X, February 25, 2024, x.com/tferriss/status/1761836093131878669.

Chapter 7

p. 206 "I wish there was a way to know": "The Office - Good Old Days - Andy Bernard," posted January 10, 2019, by Kyle, YouTube, youtube.com/watch?v=ujJQyhB0dws.

p. 208 *"Life moves pretty fast . . . you could miss it"*: *Ferris Bueller's Day Off*, directed by John Hughes (Paramount Pictures, 1986).

p. 209 *Martin Seligman once ran an experiment*: "Learned Helplessness," *Simply Psychology*, simplypsychology.org/learned-helplessness.html.

p. 210 *"Your calendar tells you what is important to you"*: MBS is a friend and the man behind the bestseller *The Coaching Habit*. I highly recommend his newsletter. Michael Bungay Stanier, "Creating Your Life: Time & Temperature," MBS Works, January 23, 2024, mbs.works/the-works-creating-your-life-time-temperature.

p. 211 *"Vacations are great, but do you know what's even greater?"*: Ryan Holiday (@RyanHoliday), X, August 11, 2024, x.com/RyanHoliday/status/1690030317531467776.

p. 219 *"My mission in life"*: Maya Angelou (@MayaAngelou), Facebook, July 5, 2011, facebook.com/MayaAngelou/posts/10150251846629796.

p. 213 *"Exercise forgives a lot of sins"*: "Stuart Phillips, PhD, on Building Muscle with Resistance Exercise and Reassessing Protein Intake," interview by Rhonda Patrick, posted June 29, 2022, by FoundMyFitness, YouTube, youtube.com/watch?v=r8DSpOd0NZc.

p. 223 *To change one's life: Start immediately*: Jessica Lamb-Shapiro, "What Would William James Do?" *HuffPost*, February 12, 2015, huffpost.com/entry/what-would-william-james-do_b_6654846.

p. 229 *"Today was good. Today was fun"*: Dr. Seuss, *One Fish Two Fish Red Fish Blue Fish* (Beginner Books, 1960).

RESOURCES

Below is a list of sources that have inspired me throughout my career and contributed to the ideas in this book. If you're looking for what's next, any of these are great stepping stones on the path to more joy in work and life:

On reimagining work

Out of Office (design lab and platform), Alice Katter

Work for Humans (podcast), Dart Lindsley

On creative confidence and brilliant work

Upfront (community and platform), Lauren Currie OBE

The War of Art, Steven Pressfield

Slow Productivity, Cal Newport

On taking care of your Stradivarius

FoundMyFitness (podcast and platform), Dr. Rhonda Patrick

Outlive, Dr. Peter Attia

On keeping it cool

Meditations, Marcus Aurelius

Tiny Beautiful Things, Cheryl Strayed

The Obstacle Is the Way, Ryan Holiday

The Happiness Trap, Russ Harris

On overwork and using our time wisely

The Good Enough Job, Simone Stolzoff

On the Shortness of Life, Seneca

Culture Study (Substack), Anne Helen Petersen

Four Thousand Weeks, Oliver Burkeman

On slowing down and seeing the beauty in the world

New and Selected Poems, Mary Oliver

365 Ways to Have a Good Day, Ian Sanders

ABOUT BREE GROFF

If you read the book, you know all about me, my affinity for stretchy pants, my beef with corporate jargon, and my dream of more good days at work for more people. If you haven't read the book and you're wondering who I am and if I know my shit, well that's a fair question! Here are my credentials:

- I wrote a book, but you probably gleaned that.
- I am a senior advisor to SYPartners, a 30-year-old global transformation consultancy.
- I've had the honor of partnering with C-suite leaders at Pfizer, Microsoft, Calvin Klein, Atlassian, Hilton, and Alphabet, among many others.
- I was previously the CEO of NOBL, a global consultancy pioneering new ways of working.
- I have an MS in learning and organizational change from Northwestern University and a BA from the University of Pennsylvania.
- I have delivered dozens of keynotes around the world, from NYC to Stockholm to Lima to Zoom, on the human experience of work.
- I had a few fun career adventures before consulting, including founding an innovation function, conducting research on body language at a dating app company, teaching middle and high school math and physics, and very unsuccessfully acting in LA when I was 23.
- I live with my husband, Brad, and daughter, Arden, in NYC.
- When I'm stressed, my motto is "most things, most days," and sometimes that even means ending my day in bed eating takeout queso and watching reality TV. But most days, I'm healthy. Most days, I'm happy. Most days, I have a really, really good time at work.

WHAT DO WE DO NOW?

Well, if you're up for it, we spread the word!

Leave an online review: I've heard writing reviews is basically the definition of fun. Would you be so kind as to leave me one via your favorite online retailer or book review site? It makes a big difference and would mean a lot to me.

Share a picture: It would totally make my heart sing if you'd also be kind enough to share a picture of the book (or ideally your gorgeous face and the book) on LinkedIn or your platform of choice and tag me. I'm so ready to go like that post!

Bring more good days to your team: If you want to buy copies for your team and discuss it together, email the receipt of your team book purchase to todaywasfun@breegroff.com. I'll send you a deck that will lead you through the discussion, along with my most enthusiastic virtual high five.

Bring more good days to your organization: If you want copies for your whole organization, that's so cool! Contact me for a bulk discount at bree@breegroff.com. It's possible to do fun things like include a foreword from your CEO in the book, and I'm happy to write your organization a little love letter too after a call to learn more about you.

Bring me to a stage: I never fulfilled my early 20s dream of becoming a famous actor… turns out I was destined for the corporate stage! If you'd like me to speak at your organization or event, reach out to me at bree@breegroff.com. I should note that in order to keep speaking a source of joy AND be one of many in my life, I'm a bit selective about the engagements I take on.

"Bree is a modern-day Renaissance woman: a real pioneer for businesses, for people and society. Bree rewires the world's largest businesses, their teams, and the skeptical minds of their leaders by practically showing them how a company could be run in a soulful, purposeful, authentic, collaborative, and human way—what we all deeply long for!—while consistently producing tremendous performance. While others talk or write about transformation, Bree is one of the few in the world who has cracked the code in delivering next-generation workplaces people simply love being part of. At several of our events around the world (London, San Diego, Stockholm), Bree was the most praised and inspiring speaker. Her speeches bring about immediate action. If there is one individual on this planet you need in your business now, it is Bree. She will make it better in every (un)thinkable way!"

TONY MARKOVSKI, managing director, Xynteo

(Thank you, Tony!)

Scattered numbers, placed with care

A hidden message, if you dare

Trade each one for letters true

And find the note I left for you ☺